A simple and elegant system for organization.
David Pearson, COO, Vistage Wor̶ ̶ ̶ ̶, ̶ ̶ ̶ ̶.

Easy to learn, train, execute, and measure individual performance.
Pete Flath, Director, Customer Success, Salesforce

Simple and approachable; exactly what to do to elevate your sales performance.
Jason Jordan, Partner, Vantage Point Performance, and author of *Cracking The Sales Management Code*: The Secrets to Measuring and Managing Sales Performance

Easy-to-read and immediately actionable framework to up your game.
Nick Miller, President, Clarity Advantage

Valuable new insights into the selling process. An implementable, repeatable, and highly effective sales methodology.
Tim Owen, Founder & CEO, NeuroCrunch LLC

I highly recommend that you embrace Level Five Selling into your best practices.
Michael G. Vicari, Chief Commercial Officer, True Health Diagnostics

Straightforward and comprehensive, yet easy to grasp and even easier to remember. This book puts things in the most clear and concise manner yet.
TJ Protsman, Director of Sales, Learning Environments, One Workplace

An easy-to-understand yet powerful model to increase the quality of your sales calls.
Cindy Domanowski, Sales Performance Consultant & Coach, Percio Strategies

Provides a clear roadmap for a sales leader to build high sales performance within a very short period.
Jerry Bevers, Senior Banking Consultant, Mortgage Banking

ISBN: 978-1-64184-196-2   Paperback
        978-1-64184-197-9   ebook

Praise for *Level Five Coaching*

Puts the science of selling into layman's terms, providing a clear understanding of how to sell well.
Tom Hopkins, author of *How to Master the Art of Selling* and *When Buyers Say No*

Inspires even sales stars to superior performance levels and provides the illusive competitive edge in closing large global deals.
Michael A. Rosinski, President & CEO, Astoria Software

A critical tool to measure the effectiveness of a company's sales force.
Jim Schneider, SCRP, Executive VP, Business Development, Weichert Workforce Mobility Inc.

The Level Five Selling implementation methods, measurement tools, and manager evaluation processes will move your team to a new level!
Kevin Pratt, VP of Sales, Tear Film Innovations, Inc.

This clear and actionable approach provides a framework against which every salesperson and sales leader can benchmark.
Kim Capps, CEO, InsideOut Development

A guide to elevate the performance of your sales force.
Jim Lennertz, Senior VP EUMEA Commercial Operations and GM BioMarin International Limited

A framework that presents sales leadership an actionable path forward for building a superior sales team.
Janet Spirer, Founder, Sales Momentum

Be prepared to grow!
Leo Pusateri, President & Owner of Pusateri Consulting, and author of *Mirror Mirror on the Wall Am I The Most Valued of Them All?* and *You Are the Value*

Simple concepts and practical approaches easily applied to drive sales growth and profitability.
Rick Beller, Global President and COO, The History Factory

Simple and ingenious. You'll see your sales will go up.
Rex Brown, President, Get Client Access

An easily understood model that enables sales managers to develop and coach their salespeople to be top performers.
Christopher Rice, former President & CEO of BlessingWhite, and author of
The Engagement Equation: Leadership Strategies for an Inspired Workforce

Real-world leadership experience; a succinct plan to create a lasting, high-performing sales organization.
Mike Monson, Outside Sales Account Manager II, Univar

I love this quote: *Level Five reps are welcome guests because they understand the customer's unique business model, their industry, and even the customer's customers.*
Bobby Martin, Active Chairman & President, Vertical IQ, and author of
The Hockey Stick Principles: The 4 Key Stages to Entrepreneurial Success

Helps everyone from the beginner to the experienced professional look in the mirror and G.R.O.W.!
Alan Fine, Founder and President, InsideOut Development

Separates the average from the exceptional sales performance. If you seek sales greatness, you have to read *Level Five Selling*.
Jim Haudan, CEO, Root Inc., and author of *The Art of Engagement*

Brings insightful perspective to the most fundamental function.
Mark Sellers, CEO, Breakthrough Sales Performance LLC, and author of
The Funnel Principle, **a Marketo Book Club favorite**

A clear, concise, and sensible perspective for sales professionals.
Dave Stein, author of *Beyond the Sales Process: 12 Proven Strategies for a Customer-Driven World*

An action-oriented framework for sales.
John Stuart, Senior Director, National Sales, Genentech

Contents

Dedication vii

Foreword ix

Introduction xiii

Chapter 1: Why Level Five Selling? 1

The Tremendous Burden of Scrap and Waste 1

Majoring In The Minor 3

More Is Not Better, Less May Be More 6

Chapter 2: What Is Level Five Selling? 11

The Genesis and History of Level Five Development..........11

A Remarkable Approach for Remarkable Performance.......12

Level One: The Professional Visitor 13

Level Two: The Price Peddler.......................................17

Level Three: The Technical Teller 20

Level Four: The Product /Service Consultant...................24

Level Five: The Value Creator 27

Chapter 3: Becoming a Level Five Sales Leader 36

The Level Five Sales Manager......................................36

Enter Level Five 37

Level One - The Buddy 38

Level Two - The Parent 40

Level Three - The Boss 41

Level Four - The Expert Coach 41

Level Five - The Partner 43

Implementation Method, Measurement, and Evaluation 47

Measurement and Evaluation 49

Why is the Level Five approach so effective? 54

Chapter 4: The Level Five Coaching System 56

The Case for Coaching 59

Coaching Importance vs. Execution 62

Serendipity Meets Opportunity 63

Enter Upside-Down Thinking 64

Building a Breakthrough Methodology 67

70-20-10 69

Structuring a High Performance Learning Journey™ 71

System Components & Process 73

Writing a Coaching Plan 77

Knowledge Resource Center 81

More About the Microlearning Modules 85

Take Your Coaching to Level Five 88

Appendix 91

Reflection Point 1
How Much Does A Call Cost You? 91

Reflection Point 2
What Is Your Definition Of A Good Call Objective? 91

Reflection Point 3
How Do You Define A Quality Sales Call? 92

Reflection Point 4
How Many Quality Calls Do You Make? 92

Reflection Point 5
What's Your Level Five Leadership Style? 93

Reflection Point 6
How Many Level Five Sellers Do You Have? 94

Notes 95

Acknowledgements 97

Epilogue 101

Dedication

My father, George William Hoskins, Sr., a talented salesman, entrepreneur, and the hardest-working guy I ever knew. He was no stranger to perspiration. His energy abounded. Thanks for your great career advice. "If you learn how to sell, you will never be without a job." You were right, Dad.

My wife, Carol, for her enduring love and support and acceptance of me as me.

My son, Ryan, who has brought our family so much pride and joy.

My sales-pro older brothers, George and Pete, whose entrepreneurial spirits inspired my own.

My best-selling author and sister, Suzanne, who lives a free and adventurous lifestyle from the written word.

My sister, Sally (1935–1976), an accomplished artist. Her work is on display at the Albright Knox and Burchfield Penny Art Galleries and in the David Rockefeller private collection.

Foreword

Two years ago, my colleague and partner, John Hoskins, and I decided to spend some time creating a company designed to help organizations install an innovative process for developing a sales team to win more sales by creating value for their customers.

We started out with an advantage because John had just published his new book, *Level Five Selling*, which was all about winning sales by creating value.

For the past two years we have worked with clients to perfect an implementation strategy for developing and coaching the skills required to sell at Level Five.

Although the implementation journey continues, we thought it was time to pause and share what we have learned to date. With that goal in mind, John put pen to paper one more time to write *Level Five Coaching System*. It's written for those who want an answer to the all-important question: *How do we implement Level Five in our organization?*

Let me set the stage. If you look back at the sales training conducted for B2B companies over the last twenty years, that landscape would look something like the following:

Most training was conducted during two- to three-day training programs. An expert trainer delivered the training using workbook exercises and PowerPoint. The sales leaders were usually made aware of the content of the program, and in some cases, they actually attended the program with their teams. Sometimes the sales leaders were directed to work with their teams to reinforce the skills when everyone returned to their districts.

So, what did we learn over the last couple of years? Given the transformational forces in today's market, the kind of sales training I just spoke of is not going to get the job done. Companies need to put in place a new and different approach for performance development. Simply doing more of the same, just a little bit better, is unlikely to produce the skill development required to successfully create a superior sales team for today's market.

Here are the specific takeaways from our client experiences that underpin the ideas explored in this new edition:

- **Takeaway 1 – Skill development cannot be an event; it must be a process.** Parachuting into a two-day training session and expecting salespeople to learn and integrate the complex skills required to create value in today's transformational markets is unrealistic. It simply will not happen regardless of how good the program and how talented the trainer. The training effort needs to be designed as a process, not an event.

- **Takeaway 2 – Coaching is not a nice-to-do; it is a must-do if any skill-development effort is to be sustained over time.** We've heard this story too many times, and likely you've been there. You go to a sales training program and the results are pretty good. Most of the salespeople take the first steps in improving their selling skills. But then you go back in three months and visit the salespeople in the field, and to your displeasure, you find that most of their skill development has disappeared.

  What happened? Answer: A lack of any systematic coaching reinforcement by the frontline sales leaders. The sales leader is the pivotal job for creating and sustaining skill development. Their most important role is providing the coaching required to help salespeople integrate and refine the skills they learned during training.

- **Takeaway 3 – Failure to leverage recent advances in learning technologies is a grievous mistake.** The days of the physical classroom being the dominant format for delivering sales training is fast coming to an end. Today, the training needs to be available anytime, anyplace. Fortunately, advances in online video-based learning have made that requirement economically and instructionally possible.

In regard to coaching, sales leaders who find themselves running out of time to coach can make use of Learning Management Systems (LMS). Properly used, an LMS can provide sales leaders an approach to augment their field-based coaching with online video coaching.

In the Level Five hierarchy of sales skills, an important distinction is made between Level Three, which is all about *telling* the customer about the value of your product's features, and Level Five, which is about *creating* value by driving the customer's desired business results.

Level Five Coaching System describes what being a Value Creator looks like and why it's so important for increasing sales success. Over the last two years, our client engagements for installing the Level Five Coaching System have yielded some great ideas for getting it right. The purpose of this book is to share those ideas with you.

Whatever your role in implementing Level Five, wherever you find yourself in the world of sales, we believe the application of the ideas explored in this second edition will help you get there.

Richard Ruff, Ph.D.
Coauthor of *Managing Major Sales*
Partner, Level Five Selling

Introduction

"In fields of specialized knowledge, we aim to render an account that is plain and simple, yet does no violence to the difficulty of the subject, so that the uninformed reader can understand us while the expert cannot fault us. We try to keep in mind a saying attributed to Einstein—that everything must be made as simple as possible, but not one bit simpler."

A Letter from the Publisher of Time Magazine, 1962

This book is written for sales leaders who want to dramatically increase their odds of exceeding their quota year after year. However, it is equally relevant for sales trainers, who want to increase the certainty of a payback on the training programs they build or buy, and salespeople, who seek to master the art of selling, earn top commissions, and enjoy the recognition associated with being number one on the sales leader board.

During my sales career, I sold or oversaw the sale of more than $350 million of licensed training and learned many valuable lessons. Level Five Selling and the Level Five Coaching System are my effort to pass along those lessons through a better, more cost-efficient, and amazingly effective way to increase the number of quality sales calls your sales team conducts. As a result, you will quickly experience increases in top line revenues, the fruits of over-quota performance, and delighted clients.

The research for validating the content is field based. It's not only the thousands of salespeople I've witnessed who embrace the concepts or the hundreds of sales leaders who choose to manage it, but the dozens of customers who acknowledge that they have seen the Level One, Two, Three, Four, and Five sales call behaviors firsthand and have a strong preference for a Level Five salesperson calling on them.

You will soon see that Level Five Selling is an elegant, simple selling model. It is memorable and repeatable. It is applied most often in B2B field sales teams but is equally powerful when developing top-performing inside sales teams and can be modified for B2C selling as well. Salespeople and sales leaders get it and apply it immediately. The really good news is that you don't need to take people away from their customers and prospects for two or three days for them to understand it, use it, and achieve sales results. Best of all, it won't cost you an arm and a leg.

Some might suggest that the world doesn't need another sales training program. In fact, many sales leaders argue that most sales training doesn't work. They wouldn't get much of an argument from me because, deep down, I know that they're right. The failure to deliver bottom-line results has more to do with training methods than program content. Nearly all sales training programs lack proper follow-up and reinforcement. Running sales training without that is what sales training icon Larry Wilson once called *throwing seeds on concrete.*

Between the ages of two and three, children develop the cognitive ability to make logical connections to understand why things happen. The child's incessant "Why? Why? Why?" questioning has a real purpose. The skill of asking "why" never leaves our subconscious. The "why" provides us a much more sophisticated understanding of how things work. Although we don't always articulate it as adults, we continue to wonder.

- Why am I in this sales training program?
- Why are these skills being taught going to help me sell more?
- Why will my prospects and customers respond better to this approach?

Most sales training doesn't work as well as it could because of an absence of context. The answer to the "why" question is missing. Context is seeing the big picture so participants know why specific skills are taught, why they are useful, and why using them leads to better sales results and more loyal customers. Yet, there is another reason Level Five Selling and the Level Five Coaching System are so powerful.

Cognitive fluency is a measure of how easy it is to think about something and understand it. The easier it is to understand, the more we believe it must be true. Level Five Selling is easy to understand and garners immediate buy-in from sales leaders and salespeople.

Level Five Selling and the Level Five Coaching System aren't flash-in-the-pan concepts. They are a completely different alternative to the traditional approach to sales skills training. Think of it more as a sales management discipline than a sales training program. It provides a formula for turning any sales team into a "quality sales call machine."

Here is my promise. Take the model to heart, tailor it to your industry, product, and service, conduct the training with your sales leaders, and track the metrics we provide in the field with your salespeople. You will see a dramatic improvement in your sales results within a few months.

CHAPTER 1

Why Level Five Selling?

There are three primary reasons to implement Level Five Selling.

1. 60% of all sales calls are scrap and waste
2. Sales managers are overly focused on lagging vs. leading indicators of sales
3. Faulty metrics management drives quantity over quality sales calls

The Tremendous Burden of Scrap and Waste

Reason One: My in-field experience in implementing Level Five Selling finds that 60% of all sales calls are scrap and waste.

What do I mean by scrap and waste? The call didn't meet its objective either because an objective was never established or because the call execution skills were so dismal that the buying process did not advance. Now, this claim is not derived from a typical online survey, research, or focus groups. This is real, in-the-field research working directly with frontline sales managers and doing call observation. This means if a firm spends $10 million on sales and marketing to field a sales force to make face-to-face calls, $6 million of that spending leads to—nothing! Does that number shock you? Maybe you are saying, B.S., Hoskins, I don't have that much scrap and waste in my force. Well, hang in there with me and keep reading. I'll take you through the analysis so you can validate it with your sales managers and prove me wrong.

If six sigma standards were brought to the sales function, the single most measurable output of the sales production process would be the sales call. Regardless of the product or service being sold, the questions would be:

- How many calls did you produce?
- What was the quality of those calls? (your specifications)
- What did it cost you to make them?
- Who is inspecting that on the line?

 Reflection Point 1: How Much Does A Call Cost You?
See Appendix Page 91.

A rule of thumb in a production environment is that a higher quality input betters both your throughput (pipeline) and your yield (sales). You should build in quality at the front end of the production process. Don't wait until you have produced a bunch of widgets and inspect them for flaws at the end. When sales managers rely solely on pipeline reviews, they typically end up discovering scrap and waste. If you build quality into the front end (frontline managers on initial meeting calls with your reps), your pipeline will be higher quality, your sales leader inspectors will have a better handle on the deals in process, and that will lead to better sales strategy discussion and better forecast accuracy. Granted, there will always be some scrap and waste within the metrics of a production environment. We are all sinners and will inevitably make a bad call or two.

Imagine the tremendous upside potential in your team's call capacity. Completing even 10% or 15% more quality calls and decreasing the amount of scrap and waste will pay huge dividends. All of this presupposes that you and your frontline sales leaders have a shared solid definition of what a quality sales call looks like. Implementing Level Five Selling will do that.

There is another reason why I know this somewhat startling stat is true. When conducting workshops about traveling in the field, we always cover call-planning best practices. A good call objective is paramount; it prevents winging it. I ask for each participant to consider an initial meeting call scenario, give them a little background info, and then ask them to write a primary and secondary call objective. Guess what. The bulk of them are not good. We pause to define a good call objective. (See the Appendix.) After that conversation, I ask them to review the criteria we all agreed to and look at their own examples again.

Then I ask the big question, "What percent of the total calls made have a good primary call objective established before the call? Fifty percent? Twenty-five percent?" I get some very low numbers. Then I say, "Okay, what percent have a good primary and secondary objective?" I get blank stares. "So you are telling me that you are spending millions of dollars to produce calls and a significant portion have no stated call objective?" The blank stares turn into sheepish looks and lowered heads.

 Reflection Point 2: What Is Your Definition Of A Good Call Objective?
See Appendix Page 91.

Majoring In The Minor

Reason Two: Too many sales managers are focused on managing results (the numbers) versus managing activities and behavior.

Should sales leaders manage sales results or should they manage activities and behavior? That's an important question, and the argument for each approach continues. Many sales leaders have abdicated their responsibility for activity management in favor of monitoring sales results against quota and/or pipeline (funnel) health. This is commonly called "managing by the numbers." They view activity management as micro management. They say, "That's too much oversight for my sophisticated sales force."

In his book *Mastery*, the best-selling author George Leonard describes what it takes to reach an expert level in any endeavor. Once, while visiting him at his home in Mill Valley, he explained how those interested in mastering their craft must have a discipline about "loving the mat," a metaphor derived from his experience as a fifth-degree black belt in Aikido. Done correctly, practicing Level Five Selling with an observer taking you to the mat (field calls) is about mastery, not oversight.

This practice has been driven by the onslaught of CRM tools and broadening spans of control.

Certainly, dashboards and CRM tools are important to monitor, but relying solely on lagging indicators to manage sales is a lazy man's approach. It's like driving your car by looking in the rearview mirror. You can see where you have been, but you don't know where you are going. What you see in a pipeline is the result of what happened on sales calls months ago. If the sales results and forecast are shy of the plan, by the time that shows up in the monthly forecast, it's usually too late to remedy the shortfall. This is exacerbated because sales cycles are lengthening as the buying process includes more decision makers than ever before. This is true in nearly every industry segment.

When you manage only "by the numbers," somewhere ahead you will likely crash into a brick wall. Revenues won't flow as forecasted, and there will be no skid marks. One minute you're sailing along above plan and, in nearly an instant, you find yourself in trouble. You won't have time to react because you won't see the revenue wreck until it happens. Because you fail to anticipate the revenue crisis ahead, you wind up explaining your under-quota results to senior management at your quarterly business review. Bye-bye bonus and maybe bye-bye job or promotion.

Good friends of mine, Howard Stevens, co-founder of the Sales Education Foundation and Jason Jordan, co-founder of Vantage Point Performance, did a study and identified 306 different metrics sales managers used in running a salesforce. They fell into three broad categories:

- Sales activities
- Sales objectives
- Business results

They concluded that while managers spent most of their time managing category two and three (up to 80%), their findings suggested that sales activities was the only category their leadership could truly affect. The answer is that your frontline sales leaders are the linchpin of sales success and, properly focused, you will win.

The most often stated, least measured or tracked sales management standard is time spent in the field to ride along with sales reps. Many sales organizations set a range from 50% to 80%. This suggests the frontline sales manager has either one or two days a week when they fly the desk. The rest of the time, they should be with reps traveling on calls, pre-call planning, observing calls, and post-call debriefing.

However, in my experience, if you have a dozen sales leaders in a room and ask them to pull out their calendars and count the number of days they spent in the field over the last 90 days, few if any meet the 50% threshold, let alone 80%. On average, you might get 25% or lower. This is supported by a study conducted in 2008 by the Sales Management Association. When I ask why, I hear excuses such as, "Oh, this was an unusual quarter… We had lots of other meetings… Blah, blah, and blah." It may be true, but to me they are just excuses. Perhaps the only legitimate reason I ever heard for missing time in the field targets was that travel budgets were frozen. My thought is that if the top line were there, you would have your travel budget.

Once, in 1971, when IBM President Thomas J. Watson Jr. summoned all of the company's executives to a last-minute meeting, VP of Sales, Buck Rodgers, was late because he had stuck to his plan to meet first with an important client. When he arrived at headquarters, he discovered that Watson had delayed the start of the meeting and everyone was waiting for him. "I thought I was going to be fired," Rodgers recalls. Instead, after he told Watson what held him up, Watson told the gathering of executives, "Buck has the right set of priorities."

My advice is to help your sales leaders out of their tennis shoes and sweat suits and into their shiny tasseled loafers and blue suits again to go out and inspect your expectations for call activity and behaviors using Level Five Selling as their quality benchmark.

More Is Not Better, Less May Be More

Reason Three: The misplaced focus on call quantity, not quality.

A commonly stated maxim suggests that selling is a "numbers game." This is only partially correct. When your emphasis is on call quantity alone, it is micromanagement.

There is a perennial question posed to sales planners: How many sales calls should a sales rep make? I believe in setting call activity standards for performance management purposes and setting clear expectations. However, I suspect that much of the push for more calls stems from two sources. One has to do with the belief that the sales reps are not working hard enough. The other is that they simply are not covering their territory and, therefore, are missing sales opportunities.

The first concern is nothing more than paranoia and maybe a bit of jealousy or lore about sales reps who make big commissions but loaf or go play golf in the afternoon. These staffers should get out in the field more and follow some reps around for a while. Pick up your rental car at 10:00 p.m. at night in a snowstorm and leave your family on Sunday night a few times. That will cure your belief in the myth that salespeople don't work hard. The second issue is really a matter of proper job design and territory alignment. Of course, if you don't make any sales calls, you won't sell anything and your numbers will be abysmal. However sometimes, less is more.

Say what?

Consider a sales rep I knew named Doug, who had a territory in Wisconsin and an office in the Chicago suburbs. The organization held each rep accountable for 300 sales calls a year, an average of about 6 a week. That's not a huge number, but they were only counting face-to-face calls. This is a fault of many sales organizations in that they place too much emphasis on numbers while placing too little emphasis on quality. Doug never met that call activity standard, and yet he always made his sales numbers and earned the annual award trips.

At his quarterly business review, sales leaders one and two levels up in the management ranks appeared and the same conversation always took place. "Well, Doug, you only made 180 sales calls last year. If you made more calls, you would probably sell a lot more. You have to get that number of calls closer to the standard three-hundred."

Doug was smart; he didn't push back. He just smiled and said, "Yeah, you're right. I probably should. I'll see what I can do to move it up."

I was curious about Doug's strategy. One could not argue with his year after year President's Club performance, but I wanted to know why he made fewer calls than expected. I cornered him one day for a Chicago-style Vienna hot dog. Here's what he told me.

"My territory is so large that it takes at least an hour or more to drive to a client and, in some cases, it takes me three hours to get to an in-person call. I'm not going to book a call with someone unless I first have a very in-depth discussion with that person by phone. I need to know a lot about that prospect and his business before I head out the door. Then, I calculate how much revenue potential there is in that opportunity. If it doesn't hit my threshold, I'm not going face-to-face. Besides, as long as I make my numbers, they won't fire me. They'll ding me on my performance appraisal, but that doesn't affect my pocketbook much."

Doug was an insightful and innovative salesperson. He ran his territory like he was the president of his own business. (By the way, Doug was way ahead of his time on use of the phone. He would sit in his office with the door closed and smile and dial constantly.) Often, he was the first guy in and the last to leave. His work ethic and his skill at call activity management meant he was one of the few sales reps who could play by the "quality call" numbers and win. The lesson I learned from Doug is basic: Quantity isn't as important in sales as quality.

Yes, selling is a numbers game, but we suggest your sales manufacturing line should produce more *quality* calls than just more calls. Having a clear, shared definition and common language for describing what a quality sales call looks like is imperative. Sales leaders who fail to communicate this quality expectation do so at their own peril. More is not better.

Another analogy I heard a client express was the idea of painting the lines on a sports field. Far too often, we tell our teams to increase their activity levels, to make more calls. My client said that this would be like a coach telling his players to run more. Without staying within the painted lines, almost any direction would do the job of getting more, but they wouldn't score often or win much. Level Five Selling paints the lines for your sales reps on what a quality call looks like.

 Reflection Point 3: How Do You Define a Quality Sales Call?
See Appendix Page 92.

What Counts As a Sales Call?

While we are killing sacred cows, let's have the debate about what counts as a sales call. There is no doubt that many face-to-face calls have been replaced by online (Join.me, WebEx, GoToMeeting, Zoom) screen share presentations of slide decks. The traditional argument I hear is, "If I make a phone call, does that count as a sales call?"

I even had one sales leader recently tell me that a rep asked him if he made a presentation to six people, could he count that as six calls. Yikes! That really is an example of rearranging the deck chairs on the Titanic. There is another simple way to resolve this argument that I will share with you in the final chapter on implementation. It's a technique I've used successfully in my own sales teams and with clients, and it's nearly as powerful as Level Five Selling itself. I'll go into greater detail about implementing Level Five in the last chapter.

Start all these debates with your sales teams and sales leaders by asking a couple of questions:

- How many calls do you think we should make each year?
- How much do you think it costs us to make a call?
- How many of those calls do you think are quality calls?
- How do you define a quality sales call?
- How do you track that?

Gather a little data and maybe turn down those headlights a bit so the deer can see while answering your inquiry. Be prepared for a lot of blank stares and rambling descriptions, and there may be a broad range of disagreement about what good looks like. You can't just say, "Make one-hundred calls per year." You have to be clear about your expectations of a quality call, then set the number. If you only say you want more calls, instead of defining specifically the quality standard for those calls, you will get them—but they won't amount to a hill of beans in revenue. Discussing what a quality call looks like is a useful conversation, and you should make it clear that the call costs real money and you need to know if you are getting a positive return on your investment.

Many of our clients have produced video models of Level One through Five to illustrate the sales behaviors at each level. If we show a Level Three call to 20 sales leaders, roughly half would think it was a great call, while the other half would say it was awful. There would be little to no agreement whatsoever on what "good" looked like or why.

That means that if you have 20 sales leaders observing calls, you have 20 different opinions of what "good" looks like. That is neither efficient nor effective. Imagine quality inspectors in a production plant, all using different standards for deciding which widget will pass inspection.

In fact, fewer high-quality Level Five calls will produce more consistent sales results than making more Level One, Two, Three, and Four calls combined.

Perhaps the greatest compliment you get as a rep is when a customer leaves and joins a new company and calls you. That happens when you create real value for your customers.

I'm reminded of a conversation that took place with a client named Steve. He had emailed me to say he was moving on to greener pastures at another firm as VP of Sales. He suggested that I call him in a month or so to catch up.

Me: Hey, Steve, how's it going? Congrats on the new assignment. I've reviewed your website and listened to the last earnings call by your CEO. Sounds like a great new technology.

Steve: Yep, it really is great. Just great.

Me: How's that? You sound a little tongue in cheek. (Steve was known as witty and sarcastic.)

Steve: I was in the field for the whole week last week, four cities in five days.

Me: How did that work out?

Steve: Well, we made a ton of calls, but I'm not sure we sold a darn thing.

Me: Any Level Five calls?

Steve: No, some Ones, a few Twos, and mostly Threes. I now know why they hired me.

CHAPTER 2

What Is Level Five Selling?

The Genesis and History of Level Five Development

We often hear prospects say there are no new ideas in sales training and, to a degree, I think they're right. The ideas presented here are likely no exception to that rule, but while they are simple and well-known ideas, they are delivered in an unconventional manner. I first saw what became the framework for the Level Five Selling concept in 1990 during a presentation by one of the most gifted sales guys I ever met. Charlie was the sales pro par excellence at Xerox Learning Systems (XLS). I learned a lot about selling from one of the best in the business.

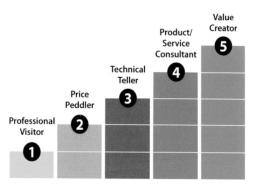

One of Charlie's greatest strengths was devising what he called an organizing principle for a presentation. He was the master of the blank flipchart presentation (today's whiteboard) where he would draw diagrams and print big bold words and arrows as he provided a context for presenting a product or service. He, along with one of his reps, had developed a whiteboard presentation as a framework for introducing the entire sales training curriculum of products being recommended by XLS. A key feature of the presentation was the illustration of a stair-step model illustrating the different kinds of reps and sales approaches that customers encounter. Their presentation was simple, easy to understand, and brilliant.

When my co-founder at Advantage Performance Group, Glenn Jackson, saw the tape, we called Charlie and Jeff to determine the source of the model. They said we were welcome to use it at Advantage, and we immediately and gratefully accepted. The stair-step concept became the centerpiece of our first direct (snail mail) prospecting effort to VPs of Sales in the San Francisco Bay Area.

This simple, one-page, two-paragraph letter with the illustration of the five-step selling ladder landed us our initial meeting calls with our first customers such as Genentech, Oracle, and Glen Ellen Winery. The feedback was consistent: "I get the model and I want my sales force to sell this way." We modified the model, added more specific content around behavior and skills, and ultimately our co-founding partner at The Real Learning Company, Richard Hodge, created a half-day training module that we sold to dozens of clients who, in turn, trained thousands of reps with it. Richard later sold Glenn and me the program as individuals to buy our stock in Advantage and become full partners. A trade that I believe he is very happy about to this day because it literally yielded him millions.

A Remarkable Approach for Remarkable Performance

The Level Five model has stood the test of time in a broad range of industries, including banks, high-tech hardware and software, consumer goods, bio-tech, medical devices, merchant card services, telecom, and even retail applications. Level Five Selling is unique in that it does not displace any existing or planned training programs. If you are using PSS, SPIN, Solution Selling, Strategic Selling, TAS, PowerBase, LAMP, Counselor Selling, Challenger, or your own sales training, implementing Level Five Selling is contextual and compatible with all of those programs. It will actually reinforce any investment you have made in other sales training.

Level Five Selling transforms the model from a sales training program to an "action learning" sales management process. There's no need to implement it as a new program or make a transition from an existing methodology to another. It is genuine, on-the-job training. There's no wasted downtime with days spent in the class-room or hours of online training. Mastery of the techniques occurs in the best environment possible—in the field. Additionally, these ideas are organized and presented by your frontline sales manag-ers in such a straightforward format that it quickly produces dra-matic results for the sales rep, the sales team, and the organization.

In the following sections, you will learn about the five levels of selling. Four of them are not up to and can never measure up to the standards required for top performance in sales. The final approach, Level Five Selling, achieves remarkable sales perfor-mance consistently and predictably because it takes a contrar-ian approach to the challenge of implementing a consistent sales methodology.

We begin with the sad tale of a famous salesman from the stage and screen, and even if the name isn't familiar, the character, his approach, and his unfortunate level of success certainly is.

Level One: The Professional Visitor

Arthur Miller perfectly described the man practicing Level One Selling in his tragic play *Death of a Salesman:*

> *"He's a man way out there in the blue riding on a smile and a shoeshine. And when they start not smiling back—that's an earthquake."*

Willy was a Level One salesman, and I think we would all agree that people do business with people they like. However, the Level One sales rep relies solely on the importance of and reliance on friendship and rapport. The salesperson is what I call The Pro-fessional Visitor. He or she is one of those people who count on, almost religiously, that people will buy from their friends, and that friendship is the basis for all buying and selling. They're often referred to as glad-handers because they're so eager to reach out and shake hands and (they think) take hold of the sales process.

The main problem with this approach is obvious. No one has enough real friends to make this concept work. Another problem is that the glad-hander approach is such a cliché that it can turn off a prospect or customer before the salesperson can begin a call.

The Professional Visitor is certainly "riding on a smile and a shoe-shine" because that's about all he can do. He probably knows just enough about his product to get by and knows little of his customer's real needs. *Why bother? We're pals. He'll give me the business*, he thinks. He's not really a salesperson when you get down to it. Regardless of the friendliness of the relationship, he is at best only an occasional interruption who drops into and out of the lives of mostly disinterested sometimes-customers.

One client described the sales rep as more or less a well-paid tourist in his territory. He has a company car allowance and an expense account for lunches and other resources for moving from call to call, but he's never really selling anything much. Generally, these reps are order takers, not order makers. They are reluctant to use closing skills because they don't want to risk undermining a friendship.

I consider myself a kind of "sales voyeur," a Siskel-and-Ebert-style evaluator of sales and service people I meet in life. You probably do the same thing even when shopping in retail. Recently, my wife and I planned to refinance our house with a competitive bank and figured it would make sense to give our primary bank a shot at the deal. On the first call, I told the AM: Here are my needs and this is the rate being quoted. Admittedly, I was dragging him into the price discussion. Here is the gist of the conversation I had by telephone.

"Because of my long-term relationship with your private bank, maybe you might be able to refinance me with less paperwork hassle and even better terms."

His first reply was this, I swear on the Bible. "So, where are you from originally?"

Shaking my head in disbelief, I asked, "Why?" I thought to myself, *What does that have to do with me getting a loan? Do I have some kind of accent?*

He simply ignored me and rolled over that question. He then proceeded to tell me he was from back East and started to chat about the current snowstorm of the century. Really? I was in a hurry with the other deal pending and his approach was candidly awkward and a real turnoff. By the way, that bank has my existing loan and the guy didn't even know the terms of that deal even though I had told him in my voicemail I was his client. Scrap and waste. His sales leader probably doesn't even know the lack of salesmanship exhibited by his team. He ended the call saying he would email the terms he could offer. When I got that email, he got the amount and the term of the loan wrong! All I could think was, *How hard could it be to sell money?*

As a mid-sized business owner, I receive calls all the time from salespeople. The question that irritates the most is this one. "So, tell me a little about your business?" I'll ask, "Have you been to my website?" Some even say, "I'm just pulling it up now." What! That's the disease I call Level One-itis and it happens every day. I know because it happens to me. Doesn't anyone out there know the meaning of "doing your homework?" Or pre-call research? Or learning as much as possible before you make the call? No excuse. No sale. The Visitor thinks he is best at winging it.

The Visitor has only one point of contact with the account, and it is generally not the owner, manager, or real decision maker/buyer. His contact is usually someone who has to get permission from a higher-up before saying yes to a purchase. The Level One salesperson probably knows about the customer's kids, but not about the customer's boss. When their contact moves up the organization or changes jobs, the point of contact is lost—and often, so is the account. The glad-hander reaches out, but there's no one there to accept the gesture.

The person practicing Level One selling rarely, if ever, develops a call plan or a well-thought-out primary call objective, so he goes in unprepared. He hasn't done the necessary homework to identify the opportunities or handle the objections offered by the customer.

Okay, I know what you're probably thinking as you read these words. *Nobody makes Level One sales calls these days. Any one operating at that level would be canned within a month in my organization.* Really? Pause for a moment and consider what you're thinking. Sadly, Level One sales calls are made every day—a lot of them. I'd not be surprised if most sales forces, yours included, waste up to 15% of their call energy on Level One calls.

The best description of a Level One call is what one medical device sales manager called the "one-song call." That's where you pull up to the account and the radio starts to play a song, you go in with the rep and the call is so short that by the time you get back to the car, the same song is still playing. They tend to use a milk-route approach to managing their territory by not distinguishing time invested with potential. A friend is a friend even if he only gives you small, infrequent orders. And that's okay with the Level One salesperson because his goal is to maintain that friendship, not to close sales. He doesn't see the difference.

If you were looking for merits, you'd say this sales rep is affable, they usually make enough calls, and, in some instances, they do have long-term relationships with buyers. Yet, there are ample opportunities to improve this rep's skill if you decide you aren't wasting your breath.

Equally sad is the fact that most of these low-end performers are never aware of this situation until it's too late and then, just like it happened to Willy, the earthquake strikes, the orders stop flowing, and a career takes a nosedive.

What percent of your sales call capacity is wasted on Level One selling? I know you hope it's zero, but I assure you it is not. Make a mental note of the percent you estimate now and we will come back to it.

Level Two: The Price Peddler

In the film *The Castaway Cowboy*, the character played by James Garner evaluates someone's manner of conducting business with the comment, "It seems to me like you're struggling your way past a dollar just to grab after a dime." That expression perfectly sums up the salesperson performing at the next level. I call Level Two the Price Peddler. I sometimes also use the term The Low Price Provider. He (or she) never considers selling the customer added value or longer-term service. They are only interested in selling the firm's product or service at the lowest possible cost.

We know that the cost, especially a low cost, is always a factor, but it's not the only factor in the decision to buy. In many cases, cost isn't even a deciding factor. The Price Peddler doesn't understand this, and his lack of understanding turns the product or service into a commodity. In his mind, the product is a price list and his approach is focused on the transaction, not the product or service, and certainly not on building a long-term, mutually profitable relationship. If you're a customer, you'll hear something along the lines of, "It's just as good as XYZ, but I can get it for you cheaper."

Naturally, the customer responds, "Well, tell me more."

You can almost hear the salesperson's inner voice, "Got 'em now!"

In working with sales and marketing VPs, we often hear them say, "We aren't the lowest cost solution, so our people have to sell value. We are the premium product, and we preach this to the force all the time. We don't want customers who are price buyers and bargain hunters. We've been training our teams on our unique value proposition and messaging. They'd better be selling our value."

Then we go on calls and watch their salespeople open the conversation with a client or potential client with such sales-killing questions as:

"What are you currently paying for your widgets?"

"You've got another loan from another bank? So what kind of rate are they giving you?"

"I know you currently use XYZ; what if I could get you about the same quality at about half the cost?"

What if the customer's challenge is a need for speedy delivery time? What if quality is paramount or service after the sale? What if the customer's real need is for a partner who can provide sound advice to help the firm increase its profits? What if a lower price is not a factor that can close the sale?

"I can get it for you cheaper" becomes irrelevant.

As you can guess, the Price Peddler doesn't create or build on customer loyalty. The concept is actually foreign to him. He sets up himself and his company for failure. Because the Price Peddler depends on a single sales feature that he perceives to be a benefit, and because he's never created customer loyalty, a competitor can come in, cut *his* price, and walk away with the business. Worse, the new guy can actually determine and address the client's real needs and the original salesperson will never be in a position to re-enter the sale. Regardless of the number of subsequent efforts, the sales calls from that point on will fall into your costly scrap and waste category.

The Price Peddler may engage in qualifying the sale, but he is only qualifying as it relates to price. I remember one VP of Sales in the consumer products industry who told me, "The price of loyalty in our business is about a penny per unit." He was referring to a fundamental law of economics (especially sales). If a customer who is buying solely on price finds a better price, you'll lose that business. Research by Hedges & Company into the price-profit relationship suggests that selling a 35% margin product at a 10% decrease in price could cause you to have to sell 40% more units to maintain your same levels of profit. Selling from price only is a fool's game.

The Price Peddler's sole strategy is to make a lot of calls. He doesn't believe it's necessary to build relationships because he's going to move on to the next customer right away. The calls are short and the reaction from the customer is equally short. Price Peddlers engage in a lot of what I call "quote and hope." They say, "Let me get you a quote" thinking that by getting a quote they've achieved a good call objective.

"Hey, how'd that call work out?"

"Oh, I'm going to deliver a quote on Monday."

"So, did you get a sense of their needs?"

"We'll know more Monday if they like our price."

"What if they don't like our price?"

"No problem. I'll go back with another quote."

The problem is that while the Price Peddler is doing busy work getting a quote or multiple quotes, some Level Five salesperson from the competition is busy closing the sale for his company. Price Peddlers spoil the market by creating market-share grabbing prices that drag everybody else into the struggle. And it's a downward spiral.

I know an automobile dealer who was once engaged in what amounted to a statewide price war between all the major manufacturers. His firm was doing well, he said, but then he added, "We're making sales, but we dealers have destroyed brand loyalty and we're going to pay for it someday." This transaction-driven sale involves very little professional selling. As a result, it never relates to larger business issues or outcomes from the use of the product and how that will help change the status quo. It's really just all about "I'm going to get you one that's as good or better, and it's going to cost you a lot less."

Often, a company will inadvertently create this kind of selling behavior with promotional efforts designed to boost sales. At that point, the rep is hopelessly dragged into the only-price-matters discussion. Eventually, however, this approach costs a lot more because it's a hard habit to break. Sales Managers I have worked with throughout the years will say that up to 20% of their calls end up in the price quagmire.

What percent of your sales call capacity is wasted on Level Two selling? Keep reading and make a mental note of that percentage, and I'll show you how to climb out of that quagmire.

 ## Level Three: The Technical Teller

A salesperson employing Level Three techniques allows his telling to interrupt his selling. You have heard people say, he "sprays and prays." He sprays out a lot of jargon and prays that something will click with the customer. Hoping to find and hit a hot button, this salesperson believes his job is customer education and there are two motivations for his actions. One, which is sound, is a belief that an educated customer will realize the value of the product or service being sold and will make the purchase. Two, he wants to show off his technical knowledge.

Think about that for a second. Does anybody really like a showoff? As with the Price Peddler, sales calls tend to be a non-interactive one-way street with the seller dominating the dialog. He slings out reams of information—not to sell, but to show the customer how cool his product is or how smart he is. The customer literally asks himself, *Why is he telling me this stuff?*

You've heard the expression "I asked the man for the time and he told me how to make a watch." It's the same with Technical Tellers. They are talking brochures.

The problem with this approach is that it rambles, and it often overwhelms the customer with too many irrelevant facts. And at some point, even relevant facts hit overload when the customer just can't take it all in.

One sales leader calls the process "show up and throw up" because the rep never takes the time to discover the client's real priorities, true needs, or wants. Without that knowledge, he has to ramble around, slinging out mostly features, few, if any, benefits, price points, and whatever else he can sling to see what (he hopes) will stick to the wall. Instead of discovering objections, a rambling approach actually creates more objections.

This is a Neil Rackham lesson from his sales research. He never had a module on handling objections; he had one on preventing objections. His cure was to ask better questions and do less talking.

Another serious problem with this approach is that it eventually numbs a customer to senselessness. You can literally see the customer's eyes glaze over. *When is this salesperson going to stop?* he thinks. Technical Tellers make the assumption that telling customers everything under the sun will reveal something that will make the customer want to buy. It almost seems like a wearing-them-down-until-they-break approach.

This is the classic situation in which the customer talks about 20% of the time and the salesperson talks 80% of the time. Or worse. A smart sales leader wants the reverse of that equation. Successful sales calls require that the customer talks 80% to 90% of the time. The salesperson should use the remainder of the time only for asking pertinent questions that add value to the conversation.

Technical Tellers are often guilty of what I call the "drive-by-shooting" sales call. It's "rata-tat-tat selling" and the aim is always off target and most of the time they are shooting blanks. "Here's all the information you need and then some... Let me know what you think... It's been great... Gotta go... See you next time." The rep is too busy talking to get any commitment to facilitate a decision.

It's even worse when there's a new product launched. They just can't wait to tell the customer all—and I do mean *all*—about the new product. Naturally, the customer is interested in any new product or service or upgrade and agrees to the sales call.

Unfortunately, what happens next is that the salesperson slips into what I call the "lecture mode" and, by doing so, creates more skepticism and indifference because of their unfocused, rambling, and fact-laden approach to selling. Again, they raise features that don't connect to needs and actually create customer resistance.

Salesperson:	"And we have a built-in fire suppressor."
Customer:	"Your widget catches fire?"
Salesperson:	"Uh, but our customer support can respond within 48 hours."
Customer:	"So, my line will be down at least two days when your widget catches fire?"
Salesperson:	"And we inventory replacement units—"
Customer:	"I'll have to spend more on fire insurance...."

I have seen sales reps feature-and-benefit themselves right out of a sale just like that. The guy who asks for the time actually doesn't care about electron flow in the workings of a digital watch. He just wants to know if he's late for beer call with the guys.

Sometimes, Technical Tellers luck out and get the sale because the product is so good it sells itself. However, in the long haul, they're still going to lose out because sooner or later someone will replicate the product or build a better one, and they'll have to sell the customer all over again. If you ask the customer, "Hey, would you like to see John again? He'll probably say, "Nah. Just shoot me a website. I'll look it up on my own." If they're dealing with a

When might a Level Three sales call be warranted?

One of our partners was calling on a VP of Sales of a Bay Area startup, a technology company that, at the time, had less than two-dozen salespeople. In kicking off the call, he asked the VP if he felt his force was taking enough of a consultative approach to their calls. The VP pounded his fist on the desk and replied with a resounding "No! They don't, and I don't want them to. We have the only product of its kind. It's breakthrough and sooner or later customers will need to buy this technology if they plan to survive. I want salespeople to go out and tell prospects about our solution and close. If the prospect is not interested, say thanks very much and go to the next call. Eventually, they will be calling us." He was probably right. Today they are F-50. But those breakthrough product sales are rare.

Technical Teller, they see no value in the rep beyond the product or service the rep carries. Again, the Technical Teller, by his own design, is little more than a talking brochure.

When it comes to call planning, go back to the idea of call objectives. Level Three salespeople tend to spend all their call-planning time focusing on what they're going to say versus what they should ask to determine how the product meets a specific customer's specific business needs. They spend their time putting together their brochures, PowerPoint presentations, and proposals and practicing their so-called pitch. As my country cousin says, this approach is "bass-ackwards." The salesperson should be investing serious time doing in-depth research and then, and only then, in planning: "What am I going to ask this customer?"

Technical Teller calls are a very shotgun, non-interactive approach. You really do see the customers' looking at their watches, tapping their feet, and drumming their fingers all the while hoping for a real salesperson to come along and address their needs.

Our experience tells us that about half the calls made today are Level Three calls. I have no reason to inflate this number. It is true. What are the odds of this type of selling being effective? We are now close to 65% of all calls being Level One, Two, or Three sales calls.

There is a magical moment that occurs in many calls with busy buyers who are distracted by the "busy – ness of business." They get past the necessary pleasantries of saying hello, turn to the rep and say, "Look, I'm sorry to be short, but I'm really swamped today. What have you got for me?"

At that point, the Technical Teller starts in with the words and jargon. He then babbles on, only to trip, stumble, fall, and lose the sale. The smart rep sees the customer's statement as an opportunity to turn the call into a Level Four or Level Five call by subtly changing the focus.

"Of course, Bob. It sounds like you're pressed for time. Before telling you what I wanted to talk to you about today, do you mind if I ask you a couple of quick questions?" Some reps will even acknowledge the "busy-ness" expressed and say, "You know, Bob, it sounds like today's not the best time. How about we reschedule when we can take some quality time to discuss what your top priorities are and how I might be able to help?"

At that point, the rep either takes control or loses control of the dialog. As they say in cooking circles, the smart rep starts to "kick it up a notch."

Let's see what that notch, a Level Four call, is like. Oh, and ask yourself what percent of your sales calls are Level Three Technical Tells.

 ## Level Four: The Product /Service Consultant

If I were to illustrate in chart form the different levels in terms of difficulty, the gap between Level Three and Level Four selling would be significant. It's a much bigger reach to get somebody who is selling predominantly at the Level Three—Technical Telling mode or below—up to the next level. The reason is that the salesperson has to start asking questions, and for most people, that's a real challenge. Reeling off memorized facts and figures while tossing out brochures or running through a PowerPoint presentation is easy. Planning and asking questions, responding to the answers, and creating additional questions, and then sales opportunities from those answers, can be a real challenge, albeit a rewarding one. I call the salesperson who can make this all-important leap the Product Service Consultant.

This is the first real level of professional selling that goes beyond just features, price, and friendship—way out of the "smile and a shoeshine" league. It's not earthquake proof, but it does put the salesperson on much firmer ground. The salesperson has the wisdom and the willingness to ask questions designed to uncover the real needs of the customer and to tie the solution of those needs with specific features and benefits of the product or service being offered. The Level Four salesperson sells solutions but not solutions to broader strategic business issues; they are solutions to tactical problems that their products solve.

He also accomplishes several other quality sales call behaviors. He knows to have a primary call objective. He realizes the need to sell to both personal and organizational needs. And he does his homework including industry and company research.

The Level Four seller has also researched the customer enough to adjust his sales style to the customer's buying style and personality. If the buyer is someone who makes decisions quickly, he's ready to act just as quickly. If the buyer requires time to contemplate a purchase, the salesperson is just as ready to exercise patience while at the same time continuing to gain momentum in the sale. If the buyer is someone who wants details and facts, the seller provides the right level of specifics to comfort the buyer. In terms of true, long-term success, he's almost there.

The Product Service Consultant asks questions, but those questions tend to reflect only the innate characteristics of their product. The salesperson tries to make a connection between a feature or benefit and something the customer needs. That's good, but not good enough. The salesperson has to answer the ultimate question: "What will this do for my (the customer's) business?" I know this machine makes 60 copies a minute and that will speed our time to complete large copying projects, but how will that help me reach my business goals quicker? The failure of the Product Consultant is going beyond the functional benefit of the product itself and describing how turn-around time is a key decision criterion when his customers select a print shop. Being able to do it faster than the competitor will help him win more jobs. They tend to fall just one step short of providing the "so what" benefit to connect to bigger picture business needs.

The Product Service Consultant reaches the first true level of professional selling but still misses engaging the customer in a more business issues-oriented conversation. While salespeople at this level will generally make quota, they are not necessarily going to be the "long-ball hitters" in the organization. They can't sell what we call The Big Idea. They can be steady performers, but they'll never reach the top ranks of sales pros because essentially the customer still sees them as just a vendor. They're a resource, certainly, but only one of several resources they could access.

The Product Service Consultant does a pretty good job, but his attitude as viewed by the customer is, "I'm here to exchange my product or service for the money in your pocket." Meanwhile, the customer is thinking and hoping, "Maybe this guy can show me how to make some more money." Level Four is a cost-level sale; it's not yet at the value-selling level a successful salesperson, sales team, or sales manager needs to achieve for true, long-term success in closing the bigger deals.

Tactically, Product Service Consultants make a pretty good call, but they don't sell strategically. They might have a few contacts in the account, but that level of knowledge and familiarity is not nearly sufficient. For example, a Level Five Selling person will rightfully try to know everybody working at the account. If you walked a customer's halls with someone performing at Level Five, you would think that person was an employee, and an important one at that. But Level Four reps stay in their comfort zone of one function. They don't venture beyond those limits. In other words, they can win the battle for one sale but lose the war for continuing sales or the huge deals.

The consultants at this level are pretty good listeners, but they miss opportunities to go beyond just the needs met by their product because in the moment they're working in the back of their heads trying to come up with what they're going to ask or say next. They think selling is like a tennis match. "I'm going to ask you a question. You're going to respond, and then I'm going to respond to your response with some product info." The "ball" goes back and forth but never gets anywhere meaningful. At least it's much better than at Level Three.

A writer/director told me that many interviewers failed to get a great story for one primary reason. They are so focused on forming the next question that they miss the valuable information being provided in the answer to the current question. By word or action, the client says, "I'll buy." But the salesperson misses the sale because he's too busy thinking, "How can I close this guy?" That happens far too many times. Product Service Consultants can also be very uncomfortable with silence in the call, and silence can be a very effective sales tool when properly used.

Comedian George Gobel defined a salesman as "…a fellow with a smile on his face, a shine on his shoes, and a lousy territory." A salesperson who can take the next step and make the leap from Level Four to Level Five Selling can turn even a lousy territory into a gold mine. I've watched them do it.

But before you move on, what percent of your sales calls are at Level Four?

 Level Five: The Value Creator

Anyone who has been in sales has most likely seen the movie *Wall Street*. In the story, Gordon Gekko, an unscrupulous corporate raider, is called on by Bud Fox, who is an eager, up-and-coming stockbroker. Fox sits nervously in front of Gekko's commanding desk. Gekko turns and says, "Tell me something I don't know." Fox finds his courage, draws on his knowledge of a company his father works for, and blurts out "Bluestar Airlines." Gekko acts on the information and Bud Fox's career, such as it turns out to be, is off and running. Gekko's philosophy, "Tell me something I don't know," reveals something important about successful selling. Level Five Sales reps understand this and bring value by enlightening their customers with things those customers did not know or anticipate in their business.

Influential research and advisory firm Forrester found that 88% of executives who have had experience with salespeople observed that while the sales personnel were able to talk about their company's products, only 27% of them actually understood the customer's business and what the customer was looking for. That further supports my 60% to 65% scrap-and-waste experience and the need for Level Five calls.

Let's reflect for a moment on the previous four levels. Each level has activities and behaviors that are strengths.

The Level One rep is good at building relationships, is service oriented, and believes he is responsible for a well-satisfied even delighted customer.

The Level Two rep has a high activity level, is often driven to achieve results, and will put in the extra effort to meet or exceed quota because he understands the math in his compensation plan.

The Level Three reps have superior product and applications knowledge, and they don't need a ton of support when the technical questions arise with the customer. They love answering the toughest questions. They can even go toe-to-toe when selling against the competition.

The Level Four reps are inquisitive about needs and plan their approach to a call before a meeting. They connect the benefits of their product to a solution the customer can understand and appreciate. They aren't opposed to closing and can navigate objections by identifying the type of resistance and ask questions to understand the real concern before responding.

As you climb the levels, you bring those good skills to the fifth level and do not leave them behind. The result is cumulative, and each level builds on the next.

We call the sales rep that reaches Level Five performance a *Value Creator*. This rep delights the customer with his or her arrival. The client subconsciously thinks, "All right! This guy's going to bring me some new ideas to help make us money." The customer thinks of a Level Five salesperson as a trusted advisor, even a partner of sorts in their business. Of course, the customer knows that the sales rep makes his calls to earn money. But the client represented by a Level Five rep also knows that the Value Creator makes that money by making the customer money.

The relationship fits the definition of a win/win scenario perfectly. The customer can't feel or say that about anyone performing at any of the other four levels. The Level Five reps are welcome guests, welcomed with open arms, you might say, because they understand the customer's unique business model, their industry, and even the customer's customers. Over time, they'll even be granted a badge to pass through security and enter the offices without screening. When that happens, you know you have arrived and earned the customer's trust.

The Level Five rep always looks at the big picture and focuses his attention on important long-term issues and priorities. His initial focus is on value versus cost because he has an in-depth understanding of the product or service, how it is unique, and the value it brings to the business. He earns a high level of respect and trust and is often invited to the planning table because the customer knows his input will be reflected in an improved bottom line.

Mark Little, a former Xerox colleague, now Principal at The Alexander Group, taught me a valuable lesson one night over a dinner in Chicago. He said that every prospect has a desire to change something about the status quo. He told me that you have to find out about their "change agenda." Perhaps the biggest difference between a Level Five salesperson and all other levels is that they discover and sell a change, not a product or service.

This rep asks intelligent and probing questions far beyond the features and benefits of the product or services he represents. He acquires invaluable information from throughout the organization because he establishes solid relationships with people at all levels and in all departments. With this insight, he uses finely honed questioning skills to uncover and even introduce the real concerns of each influencer and decision maker within the customer's organization. This level of familiarity offers benefits beyond just information gathering. The insight gained becomes a major asset when communicating with management levels—*the sales rep truly has an insider's perspective.*

Armed with this knowledge, the Level Five sales rep knows the company politics (without getting involved in them) and, most importantly, he knows where the true decision-influence power lies. He has a way of finding that individual inside who gets things done in mysterious ways, often with influence even without authority. Maybe the term "movers and shakers" is overused, but it is applicable. A Level Five rep networks alongside these people to orchestrate a decision. I recently had a VP of Sales at a large service provider tell me about a deal he did that took nine signatures for approval. Only Level Five sellers can play that game.

Value Creators work to enhance the effectiveness of the client's entire company—the totality of their organization, the team they bring together, and the products and services they offer. When Level Five salespeople arrive at a client's place of business, their thinking is focused on establishing and maintaining a long-term relationship versus only closing a sale and taking money out of the client's pocket. That's a big philosophical difference between Level Five performance and performance at the other four levels.

That point of view creates an incredible level of trust and mutual respect with the customer. That's the pathway to sitting in at the company's planning meetings. Level Five reps are viewed as people with enough strategic value to be involved in planning for the future in addition to affecting what is happening at the moment. The client actually thinks in terms of "How are *we* going to get there," with the rep being an essential element of that *we.*

Level Five sales reps adjust their selling process and style to the customer's buying process and personal style. A lot of people look at the world and think about what they've been taught in sales training: *I've got this set of steps to go through to get to a closed sale: one, two, three, close, and move on to the next customer.* The downside is that they're also, probably unconsciously, thinking, *I don't care about the customer's buying process because I've got my own selling process to go through.* If the timing isn't right, the Level Five seller will determine that quickly and not over-invest in opportunities that are never going to happen. Generally, if you ask the right questions, a customer will tell you precisely what, why, and when he wants to buy.

A Level Five salesperson realizes that there are various priorities and other concerns in the account and learns about those processes and becomes an essential element—within the process—to solving the concerns

> "Judge a man by his questions rather than his answers."
>
> Voltaire

and problems at hand. Essentially, the rep sells to the team from within the team. That's an incredible edge in making sales. When you are a rep and your key contact says, "We consider you as part of our team," you have arrived at Level Five. For example, in the health sciences field, you may even have a doctor consider a rep a part of the treatment team working side by side with the physician showing how to use the surgical robot.

Unlike Level Four reps, they'll ask questions that qualify the account in ways that go well beyond product-oriented features and benefits. They'll discover essential facts and figures about the company's long-term strategy. They'll learn about their competitors. They'll learn what the company's quarterly financial reports tell them. They develop an in-depth understanding of the customer's business. They know how that customer makes money because they know that customer and that customer's industry from the point of view of an insider. They even study the customer's customer and can show how what they sell serves those customers best interest. They are authentic, pragmatic, sincere, and serious without being solemn or "over the top" in their sales presentations.

Level Five performers are self-managed and use all of their resources wisely. My sales pro at Xerox, Charlie, once told me that people who sell at this level *"wear well in an account."* He meant that, over time, they are perceived as someone who adds value beyond their product or service and they have continuity over time with the organization. The rep calls on a buying center—IT, for example—and even though the person in that position changes over time, the Level Five person remains on the job because of his recognized and essential value to the company. Often, the rep will have a greater and more in-depth knowledge of the company than the new hire who just landed the IT manager position. And if they're selling at other levels in the organization, they're not easily knocked out of the account when somebody new comes in. They've got too many relationships built to be discarded. I've seen it time and time again. It's that "a new broom sweeps clean" mentality. But, a Level Five performer is just too valuable to be swept away.

Obviously, Level Five is the harder level to achieve. It requires you to have business acumen and financial knowledge that allows you to relate their proposals to an ROI. The classic Mack Hannan model of four ways to build value is: 1. Increase my revenue, 2. Reduce my costs, 3. Reduce my risk, and 4. Increase the certainty of a payback on my investment. Such knowledge helps the rep gain that invaluable insider position where everybody speaks the same language.

Reps selling at Level Five have real power in negotiations because their selling process creates value and they've sold value and ROI. As a result, in a negotiation, they are in a position of power because they sold and delivered value versus cost. We routinely get calls from prospects who say, "I want to train my sales force to negotiate better."

The first question we ponder is if the increased need for negotiation skills is due to an absence of good "value selling" behaviors. Which comes first? Only applying newly trained negotiation tactics to a deal when value hasn't been established won't work. Until value is established, any price is too high.

In many respects, a Level Five sales rep is a leader without a portfolio.

One big difference between Level Five and the other levels is found in their pre-call planning disciplines. The Level Five person not only has a primary call objective but also has thought about a secondary objective as a backup. Many times, when I'm delivering a Level Five workshop, I'll turn to a sales leader and ask, "What is your definition of a good call objective?" When pressed for an answer, which is a simple question to ask a rep before he goes on a call, he really doesn't have a good definition.

How can you have a good quality call without a good quality call objective? As the saying goes, if you don't have a destination or an objective, any road will get you there. Therefore, any outcome seems to be a good outcome at the time. The problem with that philosophy is that most of those roads are long, twisting, full of potholes, and often lead to dead ends. A Level Five salesperson understands what quality call objectives are and uses them to take the shortest, fastest, and most efficient road to sales success keeping the buyer's decision process in mind.

Note that we said that the Level Five rep always has a secondary call objective. "If I don't get what I want from this call in terms of advancing the sales process, what would be a backup? What could I use as a secondary objective?" He knows the answer to those questions—or at least the surest way to get them.

The Level Five salesperson is someone selling at a business concerns level, positioning himself as someone who can catapult the results that the buyer and organization are looking to achieve, and speeding the process by working with them as opposed to working with one of their competitors.

To sum it up, Level Five sales reps are experts in the industry of their client's business and the external and internal forces that drive the priorities of their buyers. Here is an organizing principle you can use to see how a Level Five sales rep goes about understanding a customer or prospect and even formulating questions for dialog with customers.

In the illustration, the bottom step represents the Global Business Marketplace that the customer operates in today. This environment is all about changes influenced by regulatory, competitive, geopolitical, economic, and technological forces. The customer's industry is impacted by these forces and reacts to both the opportunities and the risks presented by them.

The organization the Level Five rep calls on translates and responds by setting their own strategy, developing the change agenda, and addressing the business issues created in their current environment. Their position is equally one of seizing the opportunities presented or thwarting any potential threats. This establishes clear areas of focus or priorities for the functional areas that sales reps call in.

Heads of HR, IT, finance, manufacturing, marketing, and sales have a role in orchestrating the company's plan to execute its strategy. A Level Five rep positions his firm and its offerings as a vehicle to increase the speed at which that functional leader can fulfill his or her commitments to executing the organization's strategy. They present a "better way" to compete successfully and grow revenue, market share, and profits.

Although the statistics vary from company to company, only 10% to 15% of all sales reps perform at the Value Creator level. That's pretty close to the adage that 80% of sales are made by only 20% of the salespeople. The reason is obvious: only about 20% of all sales reps perform a Level Five sales call. There is a final test of the Level Five call. It is again a Neil Rackham concept. Would the customer have willingly paid for the call you just completed? At a pure Level Five performance, the odds are good that they gladly would.

Like they say in a pool hall, it's time to "rack 'em up." Let's look at your own sales team's Level Five performance.

 Reflection Point 4: How Many Quality Calls Do You Make?
See Appendix Page 92.

CHAPTER 3

Becoming a Level Five Sales Leader

"I tell my sales team, feedback is a gift, and I'm Santa Claus."

Sales VP @ Fortune Global 500 Company

The Level Five Sales Manager

During my career in this field, my best estimate is that I've made more than 2,500 sales calls and observed at least 1,500 or more while on joint calls or monitoring sales calls on the phone. This doesn't include the hundreds of role-plays evaluated in workshops. It would be fair to say that the calls fell into four categories: the home runs, the pretty good, the bad, and the ugly.

I'd like to describe a call I considered one of my home runs. Sales reps meet certain people and develop certain accounts that are more memorable than others. In the mid-90s, I had the great privilege of meeting with Mike Cheek, the President of Brown Forman Beverage (think Jack Daniels). Mike was a former sales leader at Carnation, Gallo, and Coca-Cola. He had a profound effect on me that he likely never realized.

I was selling sales training and my usual protocol was to ask about his sales managers before ever talking about his salespeople. Mike was a sage, and you just knew he was a seasoned pro. He was about to hire his EVP of Sales, Jim Bareuther, and didn't want to pursue any training until he was on board. That made sense to me, but then he said, "John, if we work together, we are going to start by training our sales managers. I want them to do three things. I want them to be recruiters, trainers, and coaches." And where did Mike want his managers? In the field, with the reps, meeting customers, planning calls, observing them, and debriefing them.

Enter Level Five

Reflecting back on my years as a frontline sales leader, Mike's statement summed up the sales managers role very succinctly. I carried that model in my head ever since, and it's paid dividends for my clients and me over and over again.

In the early 80s, a research team at Xerox set out to determine what factors made a branch office successful. It was an exhaustive study and looked at everything from compensation, incentives, and how the office was configured, along with furniture, phone systems, physical locations, and so on. After all of that investigation, they concluded one thing: If you wanted a high-performing sales team, you needed a high-performing sales manager. That was the linchpin, and I believe that to be as true today as it was then.

How does this relate to Level Five Selling? Because implementing Level Five principles is driven by the sales managers. They deliver the training and do the follow-on reinforcement. And that's just the way Mike Cheek would have wanted it done.

Level Five took off at Brown Forman as the first of what would be many programs we delivered for their managers, sales teams, and ultimately, their key distributors. We were looking for a way to have a similar model to describe sales managers and the various approaches or levels they might take to leading the sales force.

Since then, I have used this model as a context piece to position Level Five Selling and other leadership development programs with sales managers. Most sales managers are salespeople who were promoted from the field. Someone observed leadership traits, the rep expressed an interest in moving into management, and next thing you know, a sales manager is born.

As an aside, many great salespeople make the mistake of moving into sales management only to discover they hate it and they are not very good at it. Mostly, it's because the roles are as different as night and day, the compensation and reward systems are not as lucrative, and the control over the rep's own destiny is suddenly dependent on others. While for some the change of environment is a great move, a high percentage of those who do make the move will fail. I believe Lawrence Peter's *The Peter Principle* is the main culprit, but there are many reasons.

Just as you and your customers will be able to visualize your reps' predominant Level Five Selling approach, they also evaluate your Level Five Leader approach. In other words, it's as if someone showed them the Level Five Sales Leader model and asked them, "How does Sue tend to lead you? What is her predominant leadership approach?" You might

think you are at a certain level but it's worth checking.

It's worth repeating: If you want a high-performance sales team, you need a high performing sales manager. It doesn't get any more basic than that. The higher you move up the levels, the more effective you are as a sales leader, and the more loyalty and results you earn from your team.

 Level One - The Buddy

The sales leader operating at the Level One is The Buddy. I am reminded of Sally Field accepting her Academy Award, "... you like me, right now, *you like me!*" This leader believes that if his team likes him, they will perform brilliantly just for him. Most likely, they do like him, at least on some basic level. Unfortunately, the leader is confused about these beliefs. Admiration is not respect. And leadership is not a personality contest. Although it is true that a salesperson will perform better for someone he likes rather than for someone he dislikes, that performance will never be at peak levels if it is based solely on friendship. Why should it? The manager/friend will never call him on it, and the salesperson knows that. Candid dialog can harm the friendship, just as the Level One salesperson believes closing might damage the relationship.

The manager at Level One is never clear about goals and objectives and certainly not about benchmarks. After all, standards have to be met. But if a friend doesn't make the grade, things could become—uncomfortable. If the situation becomes uncomfortable, the relationship could become uncomfortable. And if the relationship suffers, so will sales because…well, you see where this kind of thinking leads—failure.

Feedback on performance is no help for the same reason. Feedback, by its very nature, must at times be direct and forthright. Again, that's uncomfortable. The Level One manager tends to let things ride to preserve the relationship and the false image that friendship breeds success. Sadly, that ride takes the entire team down the road to failure as performance problems fester and become harder to turn around.

There's nothing wrong with having a good relationship with your sales team, but it's something entirely different when you try to be one of the gang. You're a leader, not a buddy, and you need to act like it. Pardon the pun, but sales is no buddy's business.

When performance doesn't meet expectations, the conversations shift and it's uncomfortable and stressful for both parties. Steering clear of being the buddy is how you avoid the 1-800 HR earthquakes.

Level Two - The Parent

At some point, a manager will (ideally) learn that being best buddies with the sales staff doesn't guarantee sales results. In fact, being a buddy results in the opposite, and that's just human nature. The salesperson will inevitably not perform up to standards, which will be blamed on any number of challenges except the salesperson's own poor efforts. Being a good buddy, the manager naturally allows his feelings to overpower his good sense. The so-called challenges continue to pile up while sales continue to fall. The situation reaches a point where something has to be done.

At this point, the manager decides to take a more parental and nurturing approach. The two buddies are no longer equals, but unfortunately, the manager isn't equal to the task. He becomes The Parent and begins to exercise some form of oversight, an effort guaranteed to fail because the Parent can't be present all the time. The parental approach is protective, generally over-protective. The personal peer relationship may have changed, but it is still personal and still considered a major element of success. The parental approach encourages the salesperson's limitations, stifles innovation, and creates a mentality of entitlement. The Parent doesn't allow the salesperson to exercise individual action. Nothing is done without parental permission. Like the helicopter parenting of today, the performers are never allowed to think for themselves, and it stifles learning from one of the most effective instructors of all—adversity.

The bottom line: continued ineffective behaviors are not well tolerated by other family members, and the company ends up with neither the dollar nor the dime.

Level Three - The Boss

When managers finally realize that while the Level Two approach may work with kids, grandkids, and that rowdy bunch living next door, it does little for the development of adult sales professionals. Coddling will universally lead to lower productivity. At this point, managers hit the "I've really got to do something this time" point and begin instituting a command-and-control system. The Parent evolves into The Boss. "I'll cover you this time, don't worry" becomes "It's my way or the highway." Command and control become absolutes. The salespeople are not allowed to engage their creativity. Mistakes are punished. Real communication is cut off. Even parents in loving families resort to the "do as you're told" mode at some point. There is little give and take here. Conversations are one way and clipped. The Boss is known for barking orders.

Unfortunately, this approach accomplishes the little it manages to achieve by compliance with rules, regulations, and attitudes emanating from the boss and not from a sense of commitment to the organization. This is negative motivation. People perform because they're afraid of losing their jobs, not because they have a passion for the work or for success. Most ideas are driven from above, and ownership in their execution is only as good as the outcome. If that doesn't work… "it wasn't my idea!" This arcane "me three stripes, you two stripes" militaristic approach creates a culture of "us vs. them" and can quickly erode to mutiny. At this point, people join companies and leave managers.

Level Four - The Expert Coach

I call a manager who achieves Level Four the Expert Coach because he or she has the experience and the wisdom to commit to the more professional and success-creating role of mentor. The

Expert Coach observes the behaviors, skills, knowledge, and growing experience of the sales staff closely and evaluates the needs of each member of the team. The Expert Coach is accepted as an authority on sales so there can be a willingness on the performer's part to hear them out. As a good coach, he passes along his own wisdom tailored to the specific needs of specific members. This approach falls directly into the "close but no cigar" category. Its emphasis, by nature, is more evaluative than developmental.

Why? Because the Expert Coach often falls into the same trap as the boss by telling the performers what to do versus asking them what they think or feel should be done. The advice the coach provides is sound, but it is presented in such a way that the communication is pretty much one way. There is a more or less accepted mode of feedback between two people but it's not a level field. The Coach speaks. The performer listens, but, again, the salesperson's performance is based on compliance and not necessarily commitment. The sales manager may also encounter a resentment factor. Many salespeople capable of achieving real success just don't respond well to being told, regardless of how experienced a coach might be. Right or wrong, it's human nature and something that must be carefully addressed.

A leader performing at Level Four spends up to 80% of the discussion time talking, which leaves the salesperson only 20% of the time to provide input. The leader dominates, the salesperson is dominated, and the sales performance is clipped just prior to achieving real success by moving into Level Five. The lesson the sales leader at Level Four must learn is the same lesson leaders at the previous three levels must learn: A true leader must learn to "ask rather than tell." I read Seth Godin daily and he recently wrote this: "The key question isn't, what's the answer? The key question is, what's the question?"

A manager wants his or her sales force to see him at the next level so that the rep thinks, "Ah, this guy has my back, and he's going to help me understand how to make more money". That's Level Five.

Level Five - The Partner

The Level Five Value Creator sales rep has a high level of skill and ability, yet to reach that level, he needs the guidance, support, and leadership skills of a dedicated manager. He needs a Partner. A Partner in performance where the discussion is more a "we" approach versus "I" or "you."

A manager operating at Level Five realizes that he or she is a true partner with each member of the sales force. The experience the leader has must be passed on to those people, but in a timely and effective manner so it can be quickly put to use to achieve optimum results. The method best suited to pass along this information is situational and through inquiry. The managers ask questions of the performer with the goal of teaching the performer to self-diagnose and thereby improve performance. Remember, 99% of the time you are not with the salesperson in the field. Self-awareness and self-confidence flow directly from self-diagnosis.

My first exposure to this inquiry model came late in my career, and I wish it had come much earlier. Alan Fine, the Founder of Inside Out Development, an Alliance Partner of Advantage Performance Group, introduced us to his G.R.O.W. model. This revolutionized my thinking about traditional coaching and provided our clients a more fruitful and mature approach to getting the most out of their people.

The method is used to bring out the best in a sales rep's performance. The leader stimulates positive response through thoughtful questioning. Handled properly, the sales rep makes the transition from compliant to committed. Suddenly, the light bulb goes on as he realizes a new behavior or approach is, in reality, his idea—an idea that will provide a bigger payoff in the game.

This works so well because the manager has employed the "ask vs. tell" method of discussion. Ask enough of the right questions and the rep will come to their own conclusions and arrive at the right answers. More important, the rep buys in and becomes committed to the solutions found in those questions. By responding to the manager's questions, he can logically think, "We came up with that solution together. We make a great team."

The emphasis is on bringing the sales reps into the self-diagnosis and self-awareness that marks top performers. The leader's listening skills are higher. Being a Partner is not a matter of saying or even implying, "I'm the expert. I'm going to observe you, and then we're going to focus on something where you're weak."

This is the difference between Level Four and Five. The Level Four leader's focus tends to be on weaknesses and the inquiry has the intention of finding fault. The Level Five Partner is trying to focus on the strengths of the team member. He will seek the individual's positive attributes and take a more collaborative approach to developing the rep's strengths and what is called "The Way Forward." It's a more innovative mentoring approach. "We're in this together. Let's work together, and we're sure to succeed together." It's a step up from the coach/team process that's been around for so long. "We're business partners here, and we both recognize we have strengths, and together we'll achieve great success."

The only time the conversation turns to opportunity for improvement might be a "don't over-use a strength" warning. When people overuse strength, that strength becomes a weakness. It slows down work and becomes a negative. Let's say you have a person on your team who is very detail oriented. That can be a positive attribute, but when overused, it can slow down progress and decision-making. Sometimes, laboring over the font size on a PowerPoint presentation can steal valuable time from actually rehearsing before the call. You have to bring people's awareness to how there are often "dark sides" to a strong suit.

The manager who goes on sales calls has the greatest opportunity to partner with the sales rep while planning calls, observing, and debriefing the performance, especially those initial meeting sales calls. That is where the manager can have the greatest impact on the sales cycle and where the sales rep has the opportunity to demonstrate the widest range of sales behaviors. Afterward, the two can meet at a coffee shop or some neutral place for a sales call debriefing. The Level Five Sales Leader starts with basic questions. For example, a conversation could run something like the following example.

Manager:	*"That's another great opportunity you prospected. How'd you feel about the call?"*
Sales Rep:	*"Pretty good. I think the customer and I have a good rapport."*
Manager:	*"Yeah, she was very pleasant. Where do you think we were on a Level Five Selling basis?"*
Sales Rep:	*"I guess I was at a Level Three at the beginning because I did a lot of talking."*
Manager:	*"Why do you think that?"*
Sales Rep:	*"Well, I never really got to the questions we planned to ask. She said she was short of time and asked me to tell her what I had. I guess I just started talking too much about the product."*
Manager:	*"Well, your product knowledge is terrific. I wish everyone was as fluent with our features and benefits as you are."*
Manager:	*"Okay. Instant replay. Do you recall when we went through the Level Five model how you handle the customer who asks you to tell them what you have?"*
Sales Rep:	*"I could have just asked her if it would be okay to ask her a question first."*
Manager:	*"Right, that's exactly the strategy. Let's practice that so you get comfortable with recognizing when you need to take control of the call. I'll be the customer."*
Sales Rep:	*"Let's go."*
Manager:	*"Okay, I say, 'Look, I'm going into a board meeting in an hour. I've got to make this quick. How about you just tell me what you've got for me today.'"*

Note that the approach is much more open, less threatening, and ultimately more educational than situations where the leader steps into lecture mode. In this scenario, the manager reinforces strengths and immediately gets the rep to self-diagnose which leads to self-correction and ultimately greater success. I call this the difference between role play and real play. Artificial classroom case studies are okay; I've watched hundreds of them and most people moan at doing them. What I just described is real practice, in the field. Done before or after a call, it's a powerful way to anchor in good skills and make them memorable and repeatable. This is in sharp contrast to flat statements I've heard that accuse or assign blame:

"Let me tell you what I saw...."

"Do you know what you did wrong?"

"How would you do that different the next time?"

"You should have...."

"If I was making that call, I would have...."

"I can't believe you...."

These are not only ineffective, but the chances are that they'll create or build resentment and the partnership falls back to a coach-chewing-out-a-player mode. Of course, none of you managers would ever do that. We go out on what we call Six-Legged calls. That's where we observe the sales rep and manager before, during, and after the call. You would be surprised at what we see. Or, maybe not.

The Level Five Sales Leader model gives people a perspective on how sales reps might perceive them and provides a context for how they should behave to add the most value to their sales team. It may seem over-simplified, but recall the measure of a good training program is how easy it is to understand and how memorable and repeatable it is. The Level Five Sales Leader model not only helps the leader, it helps the reps establish a relationship that is more useful and productive for all.

Reflection Point 5: What's Your Level Five Leadership Style?
See Appendix Page 93.

Implementation Method, Measurement, and Evaluation

A Powerful Learning Methodology

When you have seen as many training program implementations as I have, you can recount the real successes vividly. Others had someone just checking the box. "Check, we did sales training." When the best practices and techniques stuck and made a difference, it meant measurable bottom-line results. Regrettably, and quite frankly, much of what we delivered didn't stick. It wasn't that my sales force and I didn't care about results. Of course, we did.

And it wasn't that the program content was ungrounded or that the facilitator was poorly trained as a trainer. Generally, the failure was the same. There was little, or no, in-the-field follow-up and reinforcement by frontline sales leaders. The classrooms were full, the facilitators knowledgeable and skilled, but all too often, when the training was done, the measurable results were vague. Feel-good evaluations were 4.8 on a scale of 1 to 5. But that meant nothing. Level Five is designed with that lesson in mind.

The Level Five implementation methodology is patterned after Neil Rackham's original SPIN Selling program design. I suspect that many people don't know that, in the beginning, SPIN was a sales *management* training program and not a sales training program.

My first, but not the last, experience with this rock star of sales training was in the early 80s. I was among a group of Xerox Learning Systems (XLS) sales managers who were trained by Neil in Florida at the Innisbrook Resort where discussions were held regarding XLS acquiring the rights to distribute SPIN. Mother Xerox was a big user, and XLS had the dominant share of the sales training market at the time with the PSS product. SPIN would have been the perfect fit for our product line and would have been a natural next step in a sales training curriculum. Although that deal never worked out, in 1999 we became a distributor of SPIN at Advantage Performance Group and worked with Neil to run breakfast briefings on his book *Rethinking The Sales Force*.

Neil had his overheads (with colorful overlays) cleverly revealing the research on probing behaviors. His English accent added a certain flair to his presentations. Our frontline sales leaders were trained to observe call behaviors and count them with little stick men—so many S questions, so many P questions, and so on. Then we would categorize the call outcome as an Advance or Process Continues. During a 13-week call cycle in the field with the reps, we would submit our observation sheets. Neil's team would deliver back scores for each rep indicating where the coaching focus should be for the next series of calls planned. It was a rigorous and extremely effective method of coaching a salesperson's questioning skills.

Little pamphlets were provided to enhance knowledge transfer of the content of the program. For example, if a rep had to work on implication questions (the toughest to learn) he would be given the Implication Question booklet as pre-reading before the next in-field visit. We used the process, tested it, honed and polished it, and continued perfecting every aspect until we had the program down to a science. In a word, Neil's design was brilliant. It focused on the most important and least-mastered skill in selling: questioning skills. However, it did not provide a context for several other essential sales skills. This real-world experience shaped my philosophy about best practices for doing sales training:

1. The content must be line-driven by the frontline manager
2. It must be drip-fed and cut up into bite-sized chunks that are easy to digest
3. Its focus must be on call quality as the primary outcome
4. Classroom time should be minimized
5. The focus of learning should be the in-field coaching initiatives
6. It must be an easy-to-remember, repeatable model, such as SPIN

Level Five Selling follows these design principles and delivers consistent and positive results by increasing the number of quality sales calls completed, improving win/loss ratios across the board, and increasing sales funnels. The training is accomplished through a process that documents measurable results not smile sheets and pre/post tests. This will give your training department Kirkpatrick's much sought after and rarely achieved Fourth Level Evaluation—Bottom Line Results. And the real beauty is that you can get it done at a fraction of the cost of any other training initiative. It involves real work in the field with customers and little time off from "Golden Selling Hours," a term we used at Xerox to keep ourselves focused on making calls versus other daily distractions.

Measurement and Evaluation

At Advantage Performance Group a former partner and good tennis buddy named Rob Brinkerhoff helped us create the Advantage Way™ in which we helped our clients prove bottom-line impact from their training investments. We went as far as guaranteeing the results of our training when a client would implement our process. To this day, that system is one of the best in the business for measuring and evaluation and it is still available. Tim Mooney, our Director of Evaluation and Measurement, co-authored *Courageous Training* with Rob and outlined case examples of the business results achieved when training was properly implemented.

The key "ah-ha" moment from their work for me was one of those blinding glimpses of the obvious (BGO). Ask a group of trainers this simple question: When implementing a training initiative, how much time and money do you spend before the training occurs, during the delivery of the training, and after the training is conducted? The answer to that question is typically somewhere north of 80% of their resources are spent during the delivery.

Most often, outsiders or in-house staff delivers the classroom or online content. I'm not saying that is entirely bad; it's just not as effective as when line managers drive it. But the real BGO was that so little time was spent before and after the training. Most beauty contest RFPs that my sales team and I pursued insisted that measurement and evaluation were the most important decision criteria they had for selecting a partner. The vast majority of sales training initiatives were never measured beyond tabulating the smile sheets distributed at the end of the workshop.

A Level Five implementation is entirely the reverse of the typical training model. More than 90% of the resources are spent in the field *after* the training occurs. This also sets up a reporting process that is easy to track and measure. In less than a few hours, your sales force will be applying the Level Five concepts on calls. I'm willing to guarantee it because I have witnessed the incredible success of this program many times over many years. In a nutshell, the Level Five Selling Implementation is a simple three-step process.

1. Sales Managers are trained to deliver the Level Five program content (knowledge transfer) in less than a couple of hours. It is delivered one-on-one, in large or small groups, face-to-face, or virtually.
2. They reinforce the new knowledge in the field through real world application.
3. A 90-day call observation and evaluation initiative drives measurable results in more quality sales calls, increased sales funnels, improved win-loss ratios, better forecast accuracy, and a higher percentage of representatives making quota.

Here is a sample report summary from a field observation implementation completed with a medical device organization.

Total Calls Observed

Call Type	Day One Number	Day Two Number	Total - %
New	2	7	9 - 41%
SBC	9	2	11 - 50%
NBC	0	2	2 - 9%
Totals	11	11	22

Level Five Selling Score

Overall Call Score	Day One	Day Two	Totals - %
Level One	4	3	7 – 33 %
Level Two		1	1 - 4 %
Level Three	6	4	10 - 45%
Level Four		1	1 - 4 %
Level Five	1	2	3 - 14 %

In this situation, the standard set for calls was a minimum of eight per day. They had a quota that called for them to grow their revenue top line by 20%. That meant they needed to find at least that much new business and replace any lost business from existing accounts to make quota.

Think of the rich leading indicator data you have here in just one report on two days of field observations.

- What strikes you most about this information?
- What direction (areas of focus) would you want to take while debriefing with the rep?
- Some possible areas to explore would be?
- N= New Account, NBC = New Buying Center, SBC = Same Buying Center
- Does he think he is making enough N and NBC calls to generate the new business they need to make quota?
- How much time should he be investing in the base existing accounts to maintain that revenue?
- During the 2 days, were about 20% of the calls at Level Four or Level Five? Would it be better to make fewer but more quality calls?
- Are Level One calls generally those SBC calls? Do we have enough data to know?
- This rep still has more than 82% of his calls at Level Three or below. What skills would you focus on with this rep during your post-call debriefings and pre -call planning sessions?

What bottom-line results do we want? We want to achieve more quality calls, more Level Four and Level Five calls. Instinctively we know that those kinds of calls will drive more revenue and build a stronger pipeline.

One last thought on this matter. As promised, I told you that there was a way to resolve the debate with reps about call activity management and the dreaded discussion of what counts as a sales call. This little gem of a sales management process has been embraced more by salespeople than any other tool I can think of. Again, the beauty is in its simplicity. I call it The Point System. It is especially useful when new reps start up and have very little, if any, base business in their territory.

However, I know seasoned veteran sales pros who continue to use the system even though it is not required. They do so because it keeps them honest with themselves about their own activities. It's self-monitoring and it works. If you haven't any revenue and you want the satisfaction that you are hitting numbers (knowing quality activities will ultimately lead to opportunities, contracts, and revenue), it's a way to keep yourself motivated.

List the type of activities in your sales process. For example, targeted prospecting letters, emails to key contacts, online demos, face-to-face calls, proposals submitted, presentations made face to face, telephone sales calls completed, appointments booked—even an order received or contract signed. You then apply a point value to each of them and set a weekly point target. It might be 30 or 50, depending on your industry and the type of territory you manage. Inside sales teams love this because it goes beyond the traditional metrics they are accountable for and gives proper credit for hard work. Here is a sample scorecard to illustrate how you would report the points.

Activity	Points
Letter/Phone Call to Prospect	1
Referral	1
Phone Appointment Booked	2
Face to Face Appointment Booked	2
Face to Face Meeting	3
Presentation Made/Program Demo	4
Proposal Presented	5
Leader Service Day/Program Conducted	6
Public Preview Held	7
Order Process/Invoice Out	10

I say that this is a self-managing tool because if it's 4:00 and you know you have to average ten points a day and you only have five, you get on the phone, write a few prospecting letters, or get a referral to raise your average score. Note how celebration is built in with an order scoring a lot of points allowing you to go hit the golf course that day by 4:00 and get nine in before dark.

At the end of the first month, you will have enough data to begin to see trends that are increasing the number of quality sales calls your force makes. You will also start to see a higher gross potential revenue and expected value forecast in the pipeline.

By the end of the first 90 days, you may also track the following results and be able to:

- Shorten the time it takes to get new reps productive and paying their way
- Increase the number of reps making quota
- Increase the average revenue productivity per rep
- Increase the average deal size (share of wallet) with existing customers

- Reduce the amount of scrap and waste in your call activity production
- Improve your forecast accuracy
- Improve your win-loss ratio

Why is the Level Five approach so effective?

The goal of any sales training initiative is not just changing behavior but it also must improve sales results. What we know from experience and research is that most training does not stick. The reason the Level Five initiative is so powerful is that the methodology benefits from the well-known Hawthorne effect that resulted from early studies on worker productivity at Western Electric plants outside Chicago. Essentially, it was shown that people improve their performance simply from observation. This is further bolstered by Peter Drucker's conclusions that simply measuring something will improve the performance.

The HR Chally Group, a GrowthPlay company, has conducted research on World Class Sales Organizations and why customers buy. It is predominately collected in B2B sales, but I warrant it applies in B2C as well. Their data suggests that more than 39% of a buyer's decision is weighted on the quality of the rep they see and the value they bring. This is more important than the quality of the product/service, its price, or the service quality they expect. *The sales rep is your secret weapon and the one thing your competition can't replicate.* Those customer perceptions have a direct relationship to the quality of the call the rep orchestrates and whether the client perceives value received.

In one client implementation, we went out and surveyed more than 1,200 customers for their opinions about their sales force. We had them score their sales rep against the Level Five model. The findings suggested they not only desired a Level Five rep call on them, they demanded it. Some said if you can't send this kind of talent, don't send anyone at all.

Observation leads to evaluation, which leads to measurement, and that's a straight path to sales success. But remember, it isn't enough to just do this measurement and tracking. You have to walk the talk and act like a Level Five sales leader partner to get these results too.

 Reflection Point 6: How Many Level Five Sellers Do You Have?
See Appendix Page 94.

CHAPTER 4

The Level Five Coaching System

To be candid, this book started out as a bucket-list project. After forty-plus years in the business of training and consulting with sales leaders and salespeople, I had a strong desire to share my experiences so they could survive and thrive in the sales profession I respect so much.

It had also become very apparent to me that buyers have dramatically changed what they buy and how they buy. Today, there are many ways buyers can research potential companies to decide whether to purchase their products and services. A study published by SiriusDecisions found that 67% of the buyer's journey is complete before they even reach out to sales. When buyers change how and what they buy, salespeople need to adapt how they sell. I knew the old way of training them to do that was simply not up to the speed and scale of the changes we've been seeing.

Those who've been paying close attention have noticed the same thing. They know they have to adapt and be faster on their feet. They're looking for help in how to navigate this new terrain. I regularly receive phone calls and emails from former clients, colleagues, consultants, and new readers in sales leadership and sales training asking me two questions in particular:

1. *How can you help me transform my sales team?*

    They recognize that simply selling a widget isn't going to get it done anymore—they have to create value. Serving as a trusted advisor and creating value for a company is what differentiates sales organizations now. Companies are coming to expect this from the people they buy from. So, what these inquirers are really asking is, "John, how can you help me transform my team into Value Creators?"

These readers acknowledge my point of view on the 60% scrap-and-waste factor. They get the logic that more quality sales calls build stronger pipelines, improve win rates, accelerate buying decisions, improve forecast accuracy, and grow the top line. They want their scrap-and-waste factor corrected ASAP, and they want their salespeople to become Value Creators. This is not too much to ask and is totally within reach.

2. *How can I develop a culture of coaching between my sales leaders and salespeople and then leverage that partnership as an asset in my sales team?*

The people who have reached out to me recognize the potential for something special in their sales teams. What if sales leaders served as Performance Partners with their salespeople rather than just quota counters? The dynamic of the entire sales team could measurably head in a more positive and profitable direction.

The Level Five Sales Leader model is one of the most influential components. When salespeople are coached to sell at Level Five, guided by their Performance Partner sales leaders, I've seen all kinds of good things happen.

In addition to these broader kinds of questions, I also received many requests to do keynote speeches at sales meetings or to develop a Level Five Selling sales training program. My first thought was *Of course! Why not?* But almost immediately my thought became *STOP—let's not repeat the mistakes of the past.* This led me to query those who had reached out to me about their previous experiences with sales training programs, admittedly even some I had sold them. *Why were they asking me for a new one when there were already so many out there?* Literally to a person they said, "Oh, we've done them all: Wilson, PSS, SPIN, Miller Heiman." The most recent "flavor of the month" seems to be Challenger Sale. But the funniest response I received was from a VP of Sales who said, "Oh yeah, we've had a whole parade of sales training programs here, but I can't find any evidence of any of them sticking."

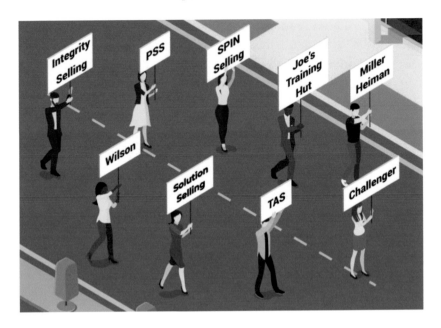

THE TRAINING PARADE

These early discovery calls with inquirers were so informative, but one of the biggest things they revealed to me was that there was a wide variety of explicit needs and cases where a new kind of system would be beneficial. Things like:

- Sales team transformation initiatives
- Transitioning from product-selling to solution-selling or when there is a portfolio of products and services
- New-product launch plans
- A merger of two sales teams from an acquisition
- New ownership from a private equity investor
- Fast growth from start-up to maturity with no common language or process for selling
- Desire to build a coaching culture
- An awareness of having underinvested in the development of sales leaders, now knowing that the frontline sales leader is the linchpin to sales productivity
- No clear direction or consistent expectations from sales division leaders

- A sense that salespeople and sales leaders were winging it

When you take all that into consideration, if there are so many sales training programs out there and so many situations that call for training and expertise, I had to ask these inquirers the next obvious question: Why did many of these programs fail to deliver the expected results?

The two most frequent responses were:

1. *A lack of commitment and buy-in from frontline sales leadership to execute.* In my experience, this amounts to a failure to inspect what you expect.
2. *Little to no coaching or reinforcement of the skills.* Apparently, companies figured if they checked the sales-training box that results would automatically follow. What they failed to consider is the amount of information that's lost when there's no follow-up or reinforcement.

These conversations propelled me on a journey to develop something new. But first I had to confirm my instincts with some facts. Was there any research out there that I could use to credential my new idea, satisfy any skeptics, and justify the approach I envisioned? I needed to be able to make the case for coaching.

The Case for Coaching

My search uncovered scores of articles and studies that backed what I already knew to be true—coaching is where the real magic happens. Here are ten of the most conclusive arguments for coaching that I found:

1. Coaching Delivers Real Business Impact

The Forum Corporation and The Sales Management Association conducted a survey recently of more than 200 companies, representing more than 500,000 salespeople, revealing that coaching is "the most impactful sales effectiveness investment."[1]

2. The More Time Coaching the Better

In their 2017 Sales Management Research Report, Selling Power wrote about how high-impact, high-performing sales organizations prioritize sales coaching and are far more proficient at sales coaching than average and low-performing groups.

They also spend more time coaching:

- 65% of sales leaders at high-impact organizations spend more than 20% of their time coaching
- 40% of sales leaders at low-impact organizations spend more than 20% of their time coaching

3. Coaching Consistently Wins the Day

Salesforce recently put out an e-book called *Five Steps to Better Sales Performance: How to Coach Your Sales Team to Higher Performance*. In it, author Amy Gallo reports that +30% more salespeople achieve quota if they are coached consistently.

The ways they recommend to coach consistently include:

- Meaningful coaching notes
- Low-friction feedback
- Clear goal-setting[2]

4. Sales Coaching Drives Goal Attainment

Salespeople who received just ten minutes of sales coaching a day enjoyed 17% higher goal achievement.

Andris Zoltners, Prabhakant Sinha, and Sally Lorimer, the authors of *Building a Winning Sales Management Team: The Force Behind the Sales Force*, found that goal achievement had a direct correlation with the amount of time sales leaders spent coaching each salesperson per month:

- Under two hours per month = 90% goal achievement
- Two to three hours per month = 92% goal achievement
- Over three hours per month = 107% goal achievement[3]

5. Focus on People, Not Administrative Tasks

According to Gallo in the Salesforce e-book, "there is a strong tendency for sales managers to get pulled into administrative activities and away from coaching and mentoring your salespeople." Additionally, she states that "sales managers who prioritize coaching over administrative duties perform 5% better than those who don't."

- "75% of sales leaders believe their front-line managers spend too much time on administration and logistics that don't add value to the business"[4]

6. Coaching Increases Win Rates

I can't address this point any more clearly than a recent CSO Insights study. Here's what they had to say about how a formal coaching system can increase win rates.

"Coaching does matter. The impact on quota attainment is remarkable, and the impact on win rates is significant. When coaching is left up to managers, quota attainment is only 53.4%, as compared to the study's average quota attainment of 55.8%. An informal coaching approach improves quota attainment to 56.4%, slightly better than average. These findings show that investing in anything less than a formal coaching approach is a waste of money.... Investing in sales force enablement to build coaching frameworks and develop sales managers, especially their coaching capabilities, is the key to seeing the kinds of performance improvements sought by sales leaders everywhere."[5]

7. Coaching Maximizes Training

According to research reported by the Corporate Executive Board in a webinar called "Building a World-Class Coaching Program," salespeople who received regular coaching from sales leaders after going through sales training achieved a productivity impact four times greater than salespeople who went through training with no follow-up. They expressed how coaching is key to maximizing the value of sales training efforts. Without reinforcement, the average salesperson who takes a course will lose 87% of what they learned within a month.[6]

8. Coaching Retains Sales Performers

The same research by the Corporate Executive Board also showed that salespeople who received highly effective coaching from their sales leaders were far more likely to stay with their company. The likelihood for one to stay at a company was consistent across all levels of salesperson performance, from low to average to high. This is extremely important because replacing an average salesperson can cost between two to three times their base salary. The cost of replacing a high-performing salesperson can be between eight to ten times their base salary.

9. Direct Reports of Effective Coaches Outperform Others

The Corporate Executive Board also found that direct reports of effective coaches outperform the direct reports of ineffective coaches by 25% and are 40% less likely to leave their organization.

10. The Most Important Sales Leader Activity

According to Forum, sales coaching is the most important of the top four sales activities that impact overall sales effectiveness. They say the most important sales activities that impact overall sales effectiveness are:

1. Sales coaching
2. Salesperson training
3. New-customer acquisition
4. Cross-selling/up-selling

Ten examples seemed ample to prove my case, but one additional study encouraged me the most.

Coaching Importance vs. Execution

According to a study from the Sales Executive Council called "Your Business Case for Investing in Coaching," where they observed 450 heads of sales and 2,400 salespeople, coaching is the activity that sales leaders perform least well. While coaching is both the sales leader activity most closely associated with salesperson success and the key to maximizing value of training efforts, it is, regrettably, also the activity that sales leaders perform the worst.[7]

While it's not uncommon for many sales organizations to profess that they prioritize coaching, not many really are—and those who are doing it don't do it very well. They feel good about purchasing the latest and greatest sales training, but they're missing the invaluable aspect of ongoing coaching. This gaping oversight gave me all the motivation I needed to build a coaching system to cure that ailment.

Serendipity Meets Opportunity

Right around the time I decided to forge ahead with building a coaching system, I had a chance meeting that created a great, new partnership. As I stood in line at Starbucks for my Grande Quad Americano, I saw a former colleague, Dr. Richard (Dick) Ruff, who was sporting a new haircut from the barbershop next door.

"Dick? Is that you?"

He turned around, smiled broadly, and said, "John, how the heck are you?"

It had been a few years since we had chatted, so we decided to find a spot on the patio and enjoy our morning brew in the Scottsdale sun to catch up.

Dick had been with Huthwaite International for many years and was also Neil Rackham's learning architect and coauthor on *The Management of Major Sales*. He had spent the last thirty years designing and managing large-scale sales training projects for Fortune 1000 companies. Those projects varied in scope from targeted sales training efforts for launching new products to international sales training engagements with organizations like UPS, McKinsey & Company, Apple, and Smith & Nephew.

Dick and I had worked together early on in our careers, so there was much to catch up on. He explained he was in the process of moving on to a new chapter. He said he felt the sales training business was, well, just different, and he was thinking of moving on, downsizing from his Scottsdale hacienda and doing more writing, perhaps of a different kind. This direction took me by surprise, so I quizzed him on what he was going to do with all the great intellectual property he had created over the years. He paused, looked up at the sky, and said, "I think I'll have a big bonfire on the beach near my San Diego place."

I gasped.

"What? No, don't do that! I'm writing a book, and I'm building a coaching system. I'm going to need IP on a variety of topics about sales."

Well, the rest is history. He called the next day and said, "Let's go—I'm in." Good fortune had once again entered my life. I'd found another great partner for a new venture.

Enter Upside-Down Thinking

In the early 90s, my co-founding partner at Advantage Performance Group, Glenn Jackson, and I would listen to *Marketplace* on National Public Radio while we were stuck in traffic in the San Francisco or Silicon Valley area. One day on the show, Glenn heard about a book by Dr. Charles Handy called *The Age of Unreason* and shared the show clip with me. Handy described a world where change was constant, random, and discontinuous. His way for people to meet the unreasoned, turbulent times ahead was a prescription called upside-down thinking. It was the notion that you had to turn ideas, problems, and things on their head in order to be able to develop a breakthrough approach.

The first thing that came to my mind was Bizarro World in the old Superman comics where everything was opposite—Earth was called "Htrae" and was square. Now Bizarro World can refer to all kinds of things that are opposite to expectations or common practice.

Then a more contemporary upside-down idea struck me. Remember the old Heinz Ketchup bottle? Think of the years we spent tapping the bottom of that bottle to get the darn stuff to flow. If that failed, we would stick a knife up the bottleneck to loosen the jam. Often, we were so successful in our efforts to get some ketchup out that we ended up spraying ourselves or others with one too many overzealous taps. Splat! I suspect that some smart product manager had an ah-ha moment and said, "Hey, this is simple. It's about gravity—turn the bottle upside down."

The Old Way   The New Way

I decided to apply the upside-down thinking technique to create a set of design criteria for building not just another sales training program but a coaching system. One that could sustain the development of sales professionals, both new hires and seasoned pros, over the long haul and help them master Level Five Selling.

As a next step, I again contacted several of the folks who had reached out to me to ask them specifically about their experience with the design and delivery of traditional sales training programs. I needed to know the shortcomings of their ketchup bottle.

Here's what I uncovered:

- **Costly, Ineffective Classroom Delivery** – They told me that the material just didn't seem to stick despite having spent a fortune on the training.

According to the early studies by Hermann Ebbinghaus and later research by Neil Rackham at Huthwaite International, we know that classroom learning pretty much evaporates in thirty days. That's a lot of time and energy down the tubes if it dissipates in a single month.

- **Expensive Travel and Time-Out-of-Field Costs** – I heard a lot about how much time was lost and that the bill to get the sales team to the training rivaled the cost of the training itself.

  When a company decides to send their sales team to a sales training program, they must take into consideration the cost of travel, food, and lodging coupled with the intangible costs of sales downtime.

- **Training Delivered by Trainers** – Salespeople reported having a difficult time absorbing the training delivered by internal staff trainers or external consultants. They'd much prefer to be trained by someone who is highly familiar with them and their situation.

- **Limited Assessment and Evaluation** – "Smile sheets" were sadly the most common form of evaluation mentioned—very much a Level One way to evaluate. Overall, the feedback I received was that very little measurement of results occurred at all.

- **Dated Learning Methods** – I heard the phrase "death by PowerPoint" more than once. I also received complaints of programed instruction reading, too much pre-work, and generic examples with little relevance.

- **Event-Oriented** – I was told about an overwhelming sense that companies had of wanting to check the box; we did the training—next! Oftentimes there was no prep before the event and no follow-up after the event either.

  It's shortsighted to assume that if you simply do some kind of sales training that you'll automatically get results.

- **Coaching was Limited and Left to Chance** – It was reported to me that participants would maybe role-play a few times in the classroom and get some feedback, but after that, there were no follow-up lessons.

That's like going to the gym to pursue your New Year's goal to lose twenty pounds and then stopping after the first class. Got it! Weight should melt off now…NOT! It cannot be emphasized enough how critical coaching is to the overall effectiveness of training salespeople.

- **Limited Practice** – So many people spoke of how little time was devoted to actually practicing what they learned.

   Mastery of any skill takes deep practice. While many professionals (musicians, athletes, doctors, lawyers) spend around 90% of their time practicing and 10% performing, salespeople tend to go for 99% performance and as a result do all their practicing on their customers and prospects. Simply put, salespeople need to spend more time practicing.

- **Sheep Dip** – Another common complaint I heard was when salespeople felt sheep-dipped, where regardless of their tenure, skill, or performance, everyone received the same sales training. They all got the same prescription of the same skills.

   Painting with wide brush like this was likely intended to not leave anyone out, but it completely disregards the individual and what they want and need.

Building a Breakthrough Methodology

With all this feedback and the upside-down thinking model in mind, I set out to build a coaching system that would get results over time and sustain the use of the skills, processes, and tools that develop high-performance sales teams. I wanted to take the ketchup bottle and turn it over.

Here's how I set out to specifically address each of the "Old Way" methods:

- **Minimal Classroom Time** – For sales training to truly be effective, we need to put the learning where it belongs—deliver it in the field.

- **Training Delivered by In-House Sales Leaders** – It's critical that we make the frontline sales leaders more accountable and responsible for the development of their salespeople. If they are required to teach the training and coach it on an ongoing basis, they will know it better than anyone and will transfer that expertise and enthusiasm on to their salespeople.

- **Ongoing Assessment and Evaluation** – Metrics matter. Use continuous quality improvement to demonstrate and yield the maximum return on investment. In addition, I also highly recommend working with a third party to evaluate results so the fox isn't guarding the henhouse.
- **Leverage Technology in Learning** – Imagine training that is available anywhere, anytime, on any device. Today, learners want just-in-time, 24/7, virtual learning tools consisting of bite-sized chunks that can be called upon in the moment. Training should be mobile and micro.
- **Ongoing Reinforcement** – Learn, Test, Practice—Repeat. Salespeople need a continuous improvement system, not a static event. It's better to drip-feed the content as opposed to your sales team trying to sip from a firehose. Reinforcing the material on an ongoing basis will help ensure that everyone absorbs the material.
- **Coaching Tracked & Measured** – When the crucial component of coaching is tracked and measured, the frontline sales leader has more control over behavior change in their salespeople, and the VP of Sales has insight into whether training is happening and how well it's happening. Once there's good insight into the program, sales leaders can add peer-learning opportunities to the mix and determine the appropriate volume of coaching.
- **Continuous Repeated Practice** – When sales leaders continuously practice with their salespeople, coaching naturally increases exponentially, all without added travel expenses. However, research shows that the coaching must be structured. CSO Insights surveyed 1,200 companies and found that the ones with a formal coaching process improved the number of salespeople making quota by 24% versus the companies that left coaching to the managers to do however they wanted.

- **Self-Directed** – Don't be guilty of malpractice and prescribe the same content for everyone hoping something sticks. Diagnose before you prescribe, and involve salespeople in the decision on how to teach them and change their behavior. They will be far more likely to buy into the system if their perspective is taken into account.

The chart below summarizes the approach to our methodology and learning design.

How To Build A Breakthrough Methodology

Costly Ineffective Classroom Travel and Time Out of Field	Minimal Classroom Delivered In Field
Delivered By Trainers	Delivered By Sales Leaders
Limited Assessment and Evaluation	Ongoing Assessment and Evaluation - ROI
Dated Learning Methods	Leverage Tech Learning
Event Oriented	Ongoing Reinforcement
Coaching Left to Chance	Coaching Tracked & Measured
Limited Practice	Continuous Repeated Practice
Sheep Dip – Double Bolus	Self Directed - Drip Fed

70-20-10

At this point, we knew the principles we wanted to teach and reinforce along with the ones we wanted to leave behind. Now we had to determine a framework for how to impart the Level Five Selling model and reinforce it. We needed a methodology and elected to embrace the 70-20-10 learning framework. In the 1980s, Morgan McCall and the Centre for Creative Leadership developed this formula. Basically, it says that 70% of learning comes through on-the-job experience, 20% through coaching or a mentoring relationship, and only 10% through formal training.

How Skills Are Mastered

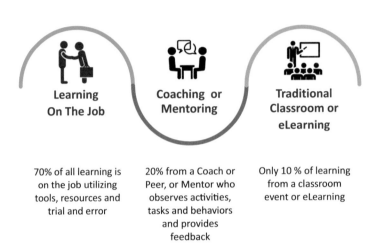

Learning On The Job	Coaching or Mentoring	Traditional Classroom or eLearning
70% of all learning is on the job utilizing tools, resources and trial and error	20% from a Coach or Peer, or Mentor who observes activities, tasks and behaviors and provides feedback	Only 10 % of learning from a classroom event or eLearning

I've heard countless stories of salespeople who attended a formal, structured class or spent time in eLearning, but when they got back to work, nothing much changed. The reason is simple: It's ineffective. Over one hundred years ago, Ebbinghaus developed what is commonly known as "the forgetting curve." He found that we lose information over time when we don't make an attempt to keep it. Our brains simply don't retain much. In fact, Ebbinghaus proved that we will forget roughly half of what we're told within an hour of being told. The key to memory recall and skill mastery is practice, ideally coupled with feedback. Classroom training is the least potent approach to mastery of a skill.

So, we've determined that classroom training is the least effective, and it's quite costly when one takes into account lost opportunities from salespeople taking time out of the field and their travel, food, and lodging expenses. But there's another big downside—timeliness. Sales organizations can't wait for salespeople to learn. If you're hired out of sync with the classes scheduled, you lose valuable time ramping to productivity. However, when a coaching system is in place, you're able to step right into an ongoing process.

Coaching and mentoring, which accounts for 20% of learning, occurs when a behavior has been observed by a peer, mentor, or coach and they provide feedback. This kind of coaching is, of course, valuable, but by far the most potent method is on-the-job, which accounts for 70% of all learning. This is the kind of coaching our system really concentrates on. Coaching on-the-job, in the field. It's where skills, tools, resources, and trial and error are coupled with in-the-moment coaching. That's where you'll find real learning, positive behavior change, and the revenue growth results associated with that change. Today's salesperson needs just-in-time tools and resources, not the traditional one-and-done, just-in-case learning events.

Structuring a High Performance Learning Journey™

With a design concept and a blueprint for our methodology in place, we now needed to build out the Level Five Coaching System components. Being able to track and measure coaching was a key design criterion, so I contacted Dr. Robert Brinkerhoff at The Brinkerhoff Evaluation Institute. Rob is an expert on training evaluation and measurement. I knew he'd be able to help solidify our vision for what we wanted to build and how we could measure the results.

He taught me about the myth of guaranteed results that's associated with most training initiatives. He also told me about the importance of not simply conducting events but rather structuring learning journeys that provided an ongoing learning-and-development path to mastery. We were convinced. We engaged Rob and his team on every implementation of our new coaching system to demonstrate business impact and continuously improve the process.

Making Training Work

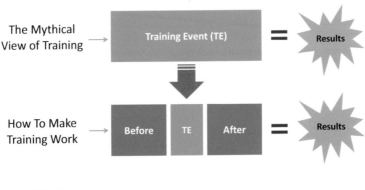

Making Training Stick
© 2018 Brinkerhoff Evaluation Institute

We had many conversations about how to make training work and came to the conclusion that it's not what you do in the training that impacts results as much as it is what you do before and after the training that matters most. With this insight, we were even more convinced to design a *system*, not a program. We built a pragmatic, easy-to-implement process, with skills and tools and a method for tracking and measuring results. Our system would empower front-line sales leaders to be accountable and responsible for training and developing their sales teams. In essence, we wanted to make coaching something that was due on Friday at five o'clock.

Ultimately, this is a change-management initiative. We were designing a system that would make fundamental changes in how sales leaders coach their salespeople. And like any change, it had to be managed over an extended period of time until it was ingrained as a way of working, not just another training program that faded into the sunset.

Rob recently coauthored a book with Anne M. Apking and Edward W. Boon called *Improving Performance Through Learning: A Practical Guide for Designing High Performance Learning Journeys*. As the title suggests, the book covers a concept called a High Performance Learning Journey (HPLJ), which they define as "a sequenced series of

In the kickoff-and-planning meeting, work will also begin on two critical components:

1. The Impact Map – This establishes the line of sight between the skills and applications of the Level Five Coaching System and the outcomes that are expected at the individual, team, and corporate level. This tool is used by sales leaders to communicate the system approach prior to individual salespeople being trained and also afterward to measure results. Brinkerhoff's research was able to document a 50% increase in "learning-to-performance" by having a sales leader meet with a participant to review this information before the training event.

Learning and Planning Workshop Outcomes	On-job Applications	Immediate Outcomes	Individual Performance Targets	Region Goals	Corporate Goals
In-depth understanding of Level Five Sales characteristics, and skill requirements Be able to: • Identify and document coaching interactions needed to set clear developmental expectations with each sales team member • Develop the skills and process for building quarterly field coaching plans for their team based on ROI • Effectively plan the visits with reps • Conduct effective pre-call briefing • Observe calls to identify sales skill strengths and weaknesses • Conduct effective post-call briefing and provide targeted skill practice • Conduct a successful Level Five Selling workshop for team.	Conduct a ½ day Level Five Selling workshop for their sales team Finalize and communicate to their sales team a 90-Day Coaching Plan Execute the 90-day Coaching Plan that will include: • Observing and identifying skills strengths and weaknesses for each team member • Guiding team members to appropriate skill building modules • Coaching each team member to improve performance • Providing coaching as needed to remediate identified gaps. • Utilize the Level Five Rehearsal Virtual Feedback and Practice Platform to increase coaching volume. Debrief and assess their 90 day coaching effort; plan their next 90 day effort accordingly Execute an improved 91 – 180 day coaching plan	Team members share a common language and understand the Level Five Selling characteristics, advantages, and skill requirements to define a quality "Value Creator" call. A plan with specific sales skill performance improvement targets set for and bought into by each team member Team members make use of provided micro learning video modules for individual learning to track skill improvement Team members continue to leverage coaching from their Sales Manager to improve number and quality of Level Five sales calls executed	FOR EXAMPLE... • XX% of team members that have received YY coaching interventions • XX% of team members executing their performance improvement plans • XX% of sales calls that meet Level Five criteria • XX% of team members meeting or exceeding quotas • XX% revenue growth in top 10-12 accounts	FOR EXAMPLE... • Grow Net Sales by XXX • Grow Gross Margin $'s by XXX • Grow Gross Margin % by XXX • Attract and retain customers • Increase Wallet Share by Product Category • Expand sales of higher margin products • Leverage the housing growth trends through increased scale • Improve sales call execution quality and effectiveness • Develop strong sales coaches	FOR EXAMPLE... • Grow Net Sales by 10% • Grow EBITDA by 15% to 20% in 2018 • Grow Gross Margin $'s by XXX • Grow Gross Margin % by XXX • Generate $1 Billion in Net Cash Flow in 2018 • Achieve above market growth in higher margin value-added products • Increased customer satisfaction and retention

2. The Customization Process – Several opportunities exist for the client to tailor the language and content of the system to fit their marketplace, including products, competitors, and customer types. Clients find this invaluable because their team doesn't have to make large leaps of faith to see how the content of Level Five relates to their world. Custom materials lend clarity to the messages and

accelerate learning transfer from acquiring knowledge to demonstrating skill.

Building a Coaching Culture

Because the focus of the system is to build a coaching culture in the sales team, we begin with a benchmark assessment of the current state by conducting a preworkshop evaluation of the sales leaders' coaching process and behaviors. This is one of several ways we measure business impact.

As a part of this process, the sales leaders complete a ten-minute online survey, which has them take a look in the mirror to rate themselves against thirty best practices represented in the "Coaching Activity Profile" below. We also determine how much time they are spending with their team and if the team feels it's adequate. We also have the team of direct reports, who are the recipients of the coaching, anonymously score the sales leader against the same thirty behaviors.

From this data, we develop a confidential report that identifies strengths and areas for improvement, which can be used as a road map for development of the sales leader. This information is vital for any sales leader, whether new or seasoned, and it also sets the example of being open to candid feedback as a team norm. This exercise gives the sales leader the opportunity to connect with their team, thanking them for the feedback and discussing how they intend to close any gaps.

Assess Sales Leader Current Coaching Practices

Coaching Activity Profile

	Read the statements below and assign a frequency value as it relates to YOU.	FREQUENCY VALUES					
1.	Give adequate notice before making coaching visits with salespeople	☐	☐	☐	☐	☐	☐
2.	Maintain adequate record of salespeople's developmental progress	☐	☐	☐	☐	☐	☐
3.	Am aware of salespeople's knowledge and skill levels	☐	☐	☐	☐	☐	☐
4.	Make coaching relevant to salesperson's individual needs	☐	☐	☐	☐	☐	☐
5.	Plan and maintain an organized coaching schedule rather than coaching only when time permits or in emergencies	☐	☐	☐	☐	☐	☐
6.	Help salespeople identify opportunities based on customer issues and needs	☐	☐	☐	☐	☐	☐
7.	Help salespeople develop strategies based on customer profile and opportunity analysis	☐	☐	☐	☐	☐	☐
8.	Ask for thorough briefing on specific accounts before coaching	☐	☐	☐	☐	☐	☐
9.	Provide useful direction in developing solutions to customer problems	☐	☐	☐	☐	☐	☐
10.	Discuss specific coaching objectives with salespeople in advance of the visit	☐	☐	☐	☐	☐	☐
11.	Indicate kinds of calls to be made during a coaching visit; type of customer to be seen, etc.	☐	☐	☐	☐	☐	☐
12.	Review specific sales call objectives before each sales call	☐	☐	☐	☐	☐	☐
13.	Establish a clear understanding of my specific role (as an observer) during the sales call	☐	☐	☐	☐	☐	☐
14.	Maintain a low profile during the sales call	☐	☐	☐	☐	☐	☐
15.	Avoid "taking over" during the call	☐	☐	☐	☐	☐	☐

Coaching Activity Profile (continued)

	Read the statements below and assign a frequency value as it relates to YOU.	FREQUENCY VALUES					
16.	"Rescue" only when needed during the call, and do so tactfully	☐	☐	☐	☐	☐	☐
17.	Let the salesperson control the flow of the customer contact	☐	☐	☐	☐	☐	☐
18.	Encourage the salesperson's input when reviewing sales call performance	☐	☐	☐	☐	☐	☐
19.	Make suggestions or explain the "right way" after reviewing the salesperson's performance	☐	☐	☐	☐	☐	☐
20.	Provide an opportunity for the salesperson to practice what's been suggested as soon as possible after coaching	☐	☐	☐	☐	☐	☐
21.	Limit the number of selling skills topics discussed at a coaching session to no more than three	☐	☐	☐	☐	☐	☐
22.	Give recognition for improvement/achievement	☐	☐	☐	☐	☐	☐
23.	Develop a specific plan for salesperson's improvement including timeframes and responsibilities	☐	☐	☐	☐	☐	☐
24.	Work with salesperson to establish practical, realistic developmental goals and plans	☐	☐	☐	☐	☐	☐
25.	Effectively communicate established standards for sales skills, product knowledge, etc.	☐	☐	☐	☐	☐	☐
26.	Give feedback frequently on ongoing developmental progress	☐	☐	☐	☐	☐	☐
27.	Make coaching a positive, motivating experience for salespeople	☐	☐	☐	☐	☐	☐
28.	Set a good example by demonstrating specific skills during the call, when needed	☐	☐	☐	☐	☐	☐
29.	Am consistent in actions, attitude, and behavior	☐	☐	☐	☐	☐	☐
30.	Have salespeople's confidence, respect, and trust	☐	☐	☐	☐	☐	☐

Writing a Coaching Plan

The next key event in the installation of the Level Five Coaching System is having the frontline sales leaders participate in a two-day planning and train-the-trainer workshop. These workshops are designed to accomplish real work. No fluff, just practical tools and skills that are used daily by sales leaders. The workshop methodology is a series of self-directed, experiential group exercises that are highly interactive and learner-centered versus teacher-centered. This means the participants are the subject matter experts, not the facilitator at the front of the room. This ensures maximum engagement, allowing the participants to draw and act on their own conclusions.

In the morning of the first day, the Senior Sales Leader (CRO or VP of Sales) kicks off the initiative with their remarks around why the organization is embracing the Level Five Coaching System and the objectives of the initiative. They should also plan to participate in the two-day workshop, not simply welcome everyone, encourage them to learn, and then leave for another meeting or even a prearranged tee time. It's critical that they drive the expectations from a position of knowing the intimate details of the system and how they work. They, too, should be coaches and follow the process and models of the system. They must also inspect what they expect in a cadence of monthly one-on-ones, quarterly business reviews, and beginning-of-the-year business planning meetings.

For the first half-day, the sales leaders will participate in the Level Five Selling workshop to understand the Level Five sales model and to take the first step in being trained as facilitators of the workshop. This is part of "training-the-trainer" because they will eventually lead the workshop for their sales team. One of the objectives of the workshop is to establish a common language for what a quality sales call looks like in their business. This includes having the sales leaders customize over forty Behavior and Characteristic Cards associated with each level of the Level Five model.

Designing Your Level Five Call Standards

In the afternoon of day one, the sales leaders learn how to build a coaching plan. Imagine the power of each sales leader planning out their coaching schedule every ninety days and presenting that completed Level Five Coaching Planner to the leader they report to. Now that's coaching due Friday at five o'clock! In this system, sales leaders will examine each of their salespeople and decide how much time they will spend with them, the types of calls they want to see, their current skill level, and the three most important skills they will focus on while traveling with them. This plan is due to their leader one week before the beginning of each quarter and should be revisited for progress checks during monthly one-on-ones. Tools like this, along with Field Contact Reports, can be excellent resources for preparing performance evaluations.

Level Five Coaching Planner

Plan Period: October 1   to: December 31   Region: Intergalactic Sample

Sales Associate Initials	Predominant Level Five Selling Approach (1 2 3 4 5)	Knowledge & Skills HI-MED-LO	Coachability HI-MED-LO	RO Priority A-B-C	Total # of Days	Types of Calls	Skill Coaching & Development Focus		
FJ	LEVEL 3	Med	Hi	B	2	New	1. Selling Against Competition	2. Handling Objections	3. New Products
JB	LEVEL 4	Hi	Med	B	2	New	1. Call Opening	2. Elevator Speech	3. Asking Questions
JH	LEVEL 3	Med	Hi	A	4	SBC	1. Penetration	2. Closing	3. Price Objections
KM	LEVEL 2	Low	Med	B	2	NBC	1. Call Openers	2. Asking Questions	3. Selling Value
TM	LEVEL 4	Med	Med	A	4	New	1. Call Objectives	2. Handling Objections	3. New Products
PS	LEVEL 1	Low	Med	B	3	NBC	1. Cross Selling	2. Call Objectives	3. Objections
KY	LEVEL 3	Med	Low	C	1	SBC	1. Call Objectives	2. Asking Questions	3. Closing
JG	LEVEL 4	Hi	Hi	A	4	New	1. Asking Questions	2. Calling High	3. Handling Price Objections
FS	LEVEL 2	Low	Hi	B	2	New	1. Pre Call Plans	2. Selling Value	3. Asking Questions
	LEVEL	Low	Low	B			1.	2.	3.
	LEVEL	Low	Low	B			1.	2.	3.
	LEVEL	Low	Low	B			1.	2.	3.

2

– 79 –

Sales Leaders Build Coaching Plans

The morning of day two, the sales leaders will learn how to execute their plans by building processes and skills for:

Pre-Call Briefings: This is the "when and what" we cover prior to making a call. These simple yet critical briefings are often a bit left to chance. However, they are an important step to having a good game plan for the call, anticipating what might occur, and deciding what you want as a result. This is a pragmatic step that sales leaders will teach to their salespeople so they can have a plan for leading the discussion on the sales call, even when the sales leader is not there.

Setting Call Objectives: Note the plural, *objectives*. We are often baffled by the quality, or lack thereof, of call objectives. Be sure to check out "Reflection Point 2: What Is Your Definition Of A Good Call Objective?" in the Appendix. This topic cannot be revisited enough. Even many sales leaders do not have a good definition for a quality call objective. We estimate that more than half of all calls made never have a well-established call objective. Essentially, a good call objective is what you plan to close on.

Observing Calls – Perhaps the most common "ding" sales leaders receive on the survey of thirty best practices is that they tend to take over the call versus keeping a low profile. This is because many have not been trained on the ways a call is structured to prevent the client from engaging the sales leader as the leader of the call. It's all about orchestrating the introduction correctly and rehearsing and agreeing to your role on the call.

Post-Call Debriefing – This is where the rubber meets the road. It's that curbside conversation or meeting at Starbucks after the call where the salesperson and sales leader discuss what happened. It's an opportunity to review what's working and what's not. Most importantly, it's a place to bring focus and intentionality to reinforcing strengths and practicing and rehearsing skills you agreed in advance to coach.

For these debriefs, we advocate a conversation process that is realistic and takes the feedback process to whole new level.

The capstone exercise of the two-day workshop for sales leaders has them practice their new skills working with three customized cases that illustrate specific scenarios from their world. After a couple cycles, the sales leaders begin to internalize the model and realize the power of meaningful post-call debriefing conversations.

Knowledge Resource Center

In the afternoon of day two, the sales leaders are oriented to the next three components of the system and the implementation process:

1. **Train-the-Trainer** – This is an exercise and introduction to the Facilitator's Guide, which will help the sales leaders become certified to conduct the Level Five Selling Workshop for their sales teams. We strongly believe in a principle of Stephen Covey that if you have to teach something, you will really learn it. That is one of the main reasons we have the sales leaders train their own salespeople on the Level Five Selling model. It also holds the sales

leader accountable for learning, skill transfer, and results, as opposed to having a corporate training department be responsible for something that is ultimately out of their control. They could put on the best training in the world, but if the sales leader doesn't reinforce it and set expectations that salespeople use the skills, then results will not be achieved.

2. **The Level Five Selling Resource Center** – The sales leaders will be walked through this abundant online resource designed for them and their salespeople. It's a compendium of more than 400 articles on all things sales and sales leadership. There are six dimensions of expert blogs and sales-related thought leadership. A simple search pulls up multiple articles for nearly any sales-related topic. It's a quick and easy way for sales leaders and salespeople to develop their skills on-the-job, just-in-time. After all, that's where most skill development occurs anyway.

These articles can be downloaded, printed, or emailed, making them great for sales-meeting learning labs. Each month, two new articles are published, adding contemporary content to continually refresh the library of articles. Sales leaders can even assign specific topics as developmental exercises for their salespeople. For example, a salesperson who is struggling with price objections can search and discover articles on pricing strategy. They can pick a couple that best fit the assignment and then present what they've learned back to the team at the weekly virtual sales meeting. Again, this resource provides sales leaders with an entire toolbox of performance enhancing resources to complement in-the-field coaching time.

The Level Five Selling Resource Center

More than 350 articles, expert blogs, and links to thought-leading content about sales and sales leadership.

Mobile ready, search and find articles related to any sales topic.

A quick, easy way to coach and develop on-the-job, "just in time" where we know 70% of development occurs.

3. Rehearsal Practice Platform – The Power of Deep, Deliberate Practice

Level Five Rehearsal™ Platform
Practice & Coaching Feedback

1
Sales Leader Collaborates with Salesperson and assigns Situational Selling Scenarios

2
Salesperson Completes Microlearning Module & Practices

- 45 Micro-learning
- 8 to 10 minute eLearning videos
- Just-enough / just-in-time training
- Personalized skill development
- Accessible through any device

3
Leader Feedback
The Coaching Conversation
Try again.
Satisfactory Completion
Or
All-Star – Leaderboard

Several years ago, the advent of online video recording and sharing entered as a new platform for streamlining the screening of job applicants. The recruiter could pose questions, and the candidate could record replies and send them back. The recruiter was then able to circulate the video to the selection team, and they would determine if the candidate should be given a face-to-face interview. This same technology was repurposed a few years ago as a training-and-development tool, and now there are dozens of virtual role-practice platforms on the market. Virtual role practice is becoming a standard in learning and practicing verbal skills and is truly a disruptive approach to conventional learning methods.

The Level Five Coaching System includes a Rehearsal platform. Rehearsal is an outstanding company that operates a safe place online for professionals to practice their skills, receive valuable coaching feedback, and collaborate with their peers and mentors. We teamed up with Rehearsal to offer this mobile-ready resource that provides salespeople and sales leaders with access to three unique features:

- **Forty-five microlearning modules** in four core performance domains: call planning and execution, account strategy, negotiation, and business acumen. It also includes video modules for sales leaders about coaching best practices. It's a mobile-ready library of best practices, all customized to your business. A salesperson could be sitting in a parking lot prior to going into a call and can brush up on any aspect of their game.
- **Leaderboard of best practice models** where exemplar salespeople who have submitted their responses to exercises are recognized for demonstrating skills they want to master. The sales leader reviews the submission and asks for permission to post the example on the leaderboard. Imagine the power of a salesperson in Jacksonville being able to watch the salesperson in Seattle introduce your new product perfectly. It's a great way for them to refresh themselves right before going into a call.
- **Channels:** This is a communication feature that allows sales leaders, and all levels, to host their own communication platform to any group of their choosing. CROs, VPs of Sales, Marketing, and frontline sales leaders can use the

tool to send weekly messages to the entire team. They can urge them to focus on specific products and clients, provide recognition to team members for performance highlights, welcome new members to the team, announce new initiatives, or even reinforce the use and power of the platform.

More About the Microlearning Modules

The modules are presented as short, ten- to twelve-minute videos, made available with the accompanying video script text. The sales leader and salesperson decide which modules to focus on depending on the individual needs of the salesperson. Each module also contains a practice assignment to confirm the salesperson's knowledge of the skill and instructions on how to demonstrate that skill using the video practice feature of the platform.

In addition to being part of the coaching effort, there other situations where a sales leader might suggest to a salesperson to review one or more of the modules.

Here are some use cases:

- When a salesperson encounters a new competitor. Watch: Winning Against the Competition.
- When the company is launching a new product and you want to practice positioning the product before calling on prospects. Watch: Understanding the Buying Process, Creating Value, or Differentiating Your Solution.
- When there is a particularly frequent and challenging objection. Watch: Managing Objections and have the sales team compile best-practices video responses.
- When the company introduces a new pricing model and the salespeople need to practice how they position the change and sell the value. Watch: the Negotiation module collection.
- When the company is going after a new-market segment. Watch: the Business Acumen module collection.
- When a salesperson needs a quick idea generator. Watch: take your pick!

The Use Case Application guide that follows provides suggested module titles for specific sales scenarios and moments that matter. A use case is a scenario you are currently facing that requires coaching and development.

Use Case Application
Configurator

	Onboarding New Hire	New Product Launch	New Competitor	Pricing Increase	New Market Segment	Tough Objections
Call Planning & Execution Skills						
1. Getting Started	✔					
2. Exploring the Buying Process	✔					
3. Building Relationships	✔					
4. Planning the Call	✔	✔	✔	✔	✔	✔
5. Opening the Call	✔	✔		✔	✔	
6. Selling Value	✔		✔	✔		
7. Asking Questions	✔	✔	✔	✔	✔	✔
8. Listening Actively	✔					✔
9. Differentiating Your Solution	✔	✔	✔			✔
10. Leveraging Storytelling	✔	✔			✔	
11. Handling Objections	✔	✔	✔	✔		✔
12. Closing the Call	✔	✔				
13. Reviewing the Call	✔					
14. Winning the Sale	✔					
Account Strategy						
1. Getting Started						
2. Reviewing the Fundamentals						
3. Improving Forecast Accuracy						
4. Selling at the Senior Level						
5. Developing Internal Champions						
6. Selling as a Team						
7. Making the Business Case			✔			✔
8. Winning Against the Competition		✔	✔			
9. Developing a Winning Strategy		✔	✔			
Negotiation						
1. Getting Started						
2. Building Trust						
3. Creating a Bigger Pie				✔		
4. Selling First and Negotiating Second				✔		
5. Designing a Strategy				✔		
6. Optimizing Profitability				✔		
7. Trading Concessions				✔		
8. Handling Deceptive Tactics						
Business Acumen						
1. Getting Started					✔	
2. Leveraging Industry Trends					✔	
3. Providing Business Insight					✔	
4. Selling Economic Value				✔	✔	
5. Know Your Customer's Story					✔	
6. Monetizing Your Value				✔	✔	
7. Preparing a Business Case				✔	✔	

10

Situational Selling Use Case Application
Configurator

	Selling to the "C-Suite"	Selling Total Value	Prospecting for New Business	Expanding Relationships
Call Planning & Execution Skills				
1. Getting Started				
2. Exploring the Buying Process				
3. Building Relationships				✔
4. Planning the Call	✔	✔	✔	✔
5. Opening the Call	✔	✔	✔	
6. Selling Value			✔	
7. Asking Questions	✔	✔	✔	
8. Listening Actively			✔	
9. Differentiating Your Solution	✔	✔	✔	
10. Leveraging Storytelling	✔		✔	
11. Handling Objections			✔	
12. Closing the Call				
13. Reviewing the Call				
14. Winning the Sale				
Account Strategy				
1. Getting Started				
2. Reviewing the Fundamentals				
3. Improving Forecast Accuracy				✔
4. Selling at the Senior Level	✔			✔
5. Developing Internal Champions	✔			✔
6. Selling as a Team	✔			
7. Making the Business Case				
8. Winning Against the Competition		✔		
9. Developing a Winning Strategy		✔		✔
Negotiation				
1. Getting Started				
2. Building Trust				
3. Creating a Bigger Pie				✔
4. Selling First and Negotiating Second				✔
5. Designing a Strategy				
6. Optimizing Profitability				✔
7. Trading Concessions				
8. Handling Deceptive Tactics				
Business Acumen				
1. Getting Started	✔			
2. Leveraging Industry Trends	✔		✔	✔
3. Providing Business Insight	✔	✔		✔
4. Selling Economic Value	✔	✔		✔
5. Know Your Customer's Story	✔	✔	✔	✔
6. Monetizing Your Value	✔	✔		✔
7. Preparing a Business Case	✔	✔		✔

Take Your Coaching to Level Five

The Level Five Coaching System is a process that includes a set of skills, tools, and resources to develop a sales team of Value Creators. It is not an event-based sales training parade but a series of learning interventions and assignments that a sales leader and salesperson collaborate on to provide a drip-fed, ongoing approach to learning, practice, and development based on the individual needs of the salesperson and marketplace.

A System to Implement A Sales Leader's Coaching Process

Your sales team is the single most potent differentiation you have against competitors. It is the most difficult aspect of their value proposition for them to replicate. The Level Five Coaching System can keep you one step ahead of them and yield the following performance outcomes and results:

+ An installed sales coaching discipline and process that will be sustained and built upon
+ More quality deals in the pipeline and improved forecast accuracy
+ Improved win/loss ratios
+ More salespeople achieving and exceeding quota
+ Shortened ramp time to full productivity

+ Reduced turnover
+ Increased customer satisfaction
+ Improved product launch
+ Double or triple the amount of coaching
+ Four to five times more practice and rehearsal of skills

Perhaps you've experienced the sales-training parade. The shiny, new program may have lost its sparkle and fizzled after a few months without you getting the results you expected. If you're tired of the same old traditional approaches to developing a world-class sales team and want to get a return on your investment in training, I encourage you to give the Level Five Coaching System a try. We are unique. Our system follows the most contemporary, well-researched learning-to-performance methodologies. Our mission doesn't end here; we will continue to enhance the system with new discoveries of the best practices for mastery of selling skills and becoming Value Creator sales professionals.

If this sounds like something you're interested in, feel free to contact me. This is something I'm deeply passionate about, and I'd love to spend as much time as you need discussing your situation and answering any questions you might have about our work. No obligation, no pressure. If my forty-plus years of experience can help you think through your sales challenges, I'm happy to lend a hand. Thank you for your interest in Level Five Selling. I hope it pays you dividends for many years to come.

Appendix

 Reflection Point 1
How Much Does A Call Cost You?

There is a number that every salesperson and sales manager in your force should know—and most do not. You must know it and communicate it to get your team to embrace Level Five Selling. *Salespeople are responsible for spending money every time they make a call and whether it's a good call or a bad call it's going to cost the organization the same amount.* You want them to know that number.

Divide the Total Annual Sales and Marketing Budget $s by the Total Number of Sales Calls

Each sales call costs us $_____

 Reflection Point 2
What Is Your Definition Of A Good Call Objective?

This is a fun exercise. Ask your team for a list of examples of good call objectives. Provide them an example scenario such as, "You are about to go on an initial meeting call for new business." You will be amazed at the variety of examples and the quality. In essence, a good call objective is what you plan to close on. And, it requires a physical action on the part of the customer. You want an introduction to another influencer, a next appointment to present a solution, gaining access to others to gather information from others you need to craft your proposal, heck, even giving you an order, if that's appropriate. If you have a good call objective, you have what you want to gain commitment to. And recall the Level Five rep has a primary and secondary objective.

List your criteria here:

1. _____
2. _____
3. _____
4. _____
5. _____
6. _____

 ## Reflection Point 3
How Do You Define A Quality Sales Call?

What criteria do you use to measure a quality call? If I were a line VP, I'd want to know—I'd *have* to know—the answers to this question. Imagine the value of having everyone in your sales force sharing a common language and understanding of a quality call. The increased awareness alone would immediately change behaviors and conversations before and after a sales call.

List your criteria here:

1. _____
2. _____
3. _____
4. _____
5. _____
6. _____

 ## Reflection Point 4
How Many Quality Calls Do You Make?

We know how much your sales calls cost and how many your sales force makes. Now the question becomes, "Are you a good steward of that asset?" I have had the opportunity to conduct this exercise with dozens of sales forces and hundreds of sales managers.

Of all the calls your entire team makes annually, what percent are made at each level?

Type of Call	% of Total Annual Calls
Level One – Professional Visits	
Level Two – Price	
Level Three – Technical Tellers	
Level Four – Product/Service Consultant	
Level Five – Value Creator	

 ## Reflection Point 5
What's Your Level Five Leadership Style?

For those of you who have been in sales management for a while, review the descriptions of Levels One through Five that follow.

Ask yourself these questions:

- If your sales team members were to evaluate you where they see you?
- Where do you believe you operate from most often?
- Do you tend to operate at the same level all the time?
- What circumstances will have you move from one level to another?
- What do your reps do that move you to specific levels?
- What does your boss expect you to do?
- Where is he or she at on the levels?

Level	They See You?	You See You?	Boss Sees Me?	My Boss Is?
Level One – Buddy				
Level Two – Parent				
Level Three – Boss				
Level Four – Coach				
Level Five – Partner				

Reflection Point 6
How Many Level Five Sellers Do You Have?

There are many possible ways to evaluate a rep as a Level Five seller. Certainly the best judge would be the customer. A manager going on some calls to observe them would be ideal, too. In the absence of that input, here is a useful "back of the envelope" diagnostic checklist to start the evaluation. Find strengths that could be passed along to others on the team and or some areas of focus for practice and development.

Diagnostic Questions
Does the Sales Rep:

_____ Research the customer's business
_____ Research the customer's customer
_____ Develop a quality pre-call plan
_____ Prepare others on the team for calls
_____ Listen well
_____ Discover desired results – product and business
_____ Identify personal needs
_____ Answer questions appropriately
_____ Know and can communicate about company and product
_____ Handle objections appropriately
_____ Understand the competition
_____ Sell value versus price
_____ Develop clear next steps in a sales cycle
_____ Provide value-added service
_____ Get closure and commitment at the right time
_____ Deliver and follow up on what is promised.

Notes

Chapter 4

1. The Sales Management Association, "Measuring Sales Management's Coaching Impact." White paper, Forum Corporation, 2014. https://go.forum.com/Sales-Coaching-Survey-Global.

2. Amy Gallo, *Five Steps to Better Sales Performance: How to Coach Your Sales Team to Higher Performance* (n.p.: Salesforce, 2013), PDF e-book, 3. https://a.sfdcstatic.com/content/dam/www/ocms/work/salesperformance/five-steps-better-sales-performance-ebook.pdf.

3. Andris A. Zoltners, Prabhakant Sinha, and Sally E. Lorimer, *Building a Winning Sales Management Team: The Force Behind the Sales Force* (Evanston, ZS Associates, Inc., 2012), 3.

4. Gallo, *Five Steps to Better Sales Performance: How to Coach Your Sales Team to Higher Performance*, 10.

5. CSO Insights, *2016 Sales Enablement Optimization Study* (Littleton: Miller Heiman Group, Inc., 2016). https://www.csoinsights.com/wp-content/uploads/sites/5/2016/08/2016-Sales-Enablement-Optimization-Study.pdf.

6. Sales Executive Council, Corporate Executive Board, "Building a World-Class Coaching Program," The Business Case for Sales Coaching, teleconference series webinar, 2005.

7. Sales Executive Council, Corporate Executive Board, "Your Business Case for Investing in Coaching," 2005.

8. Robert O. Brinkerhoff, Anne M. Apking, and Edward W. Boon, *Improving Performance Through Learning: A Practical Guide for Designing High Performance Learning Journeys* (Promote International AB, 2019), 34.

Acknowledgements

By now you have gathered that this is my first book, and I want to acknowledge and thank many of the people who helped me in my career and in life. They are too numerous to mention every last one, but hopefully you all know how grateful I am to have worked with you and known you personally and professionally.

Ron Charles, General Sales Manager at Xerox Learning Systems Canada. Ron took a chance on me. He bet on my unconventional background sans MBA from Western Ontario University or McGill. Had Ron not hired me, I would have never found my passion for the sales training world. I knew in my heart and from experience that I could sell, but then I had the gift of helping others learn to find the freedom and success that was coupled with that profession.

Carter Brown and David Bennett. We were the Three Amigos at Omega Performance Group. I learned more about training in five years at Omega than I did in nine years at Xerox. Carter and David graciously loaned Glenn Jackson (my co-founding partner) and me complete access to all resources, including offices, copiers, computers, phones, conference rooms, and more to launch Advantage Performance Group in 1990. Talk about abundant.

Glenn Jackson. It's hard to put into words how lucky I feel to have Glenn in my life. He is the eternal optimist, a gifted sales professional, decisive, bold thinking, and a continuous learner and hard worker. I love him like a brother and will be forever grateful for his partnership in business and in life.

Richard Hodge. Undoubtedly, a mold-breaking, creative genius. Richard not only has ideas but also brings them to reality. I dare say no other instructional designer had as much business savvy, sales ability, and design instinct as Richard. Glenn and I would not have thrived as much as we did without brother Richard at our side. He is the most prolific developer of training IP I've ever met and a terrific family guy, hunter, fisherman, golfer, tennis player, sailor, and I could go on. He is a very special talent and friend and a guy who will have your back.

Co-founding partners, Ed Shineman and Bob Conti, for their friendship and support in launching SalesGenomix, LLC.

The Advantage Franchise Partner and Facilitator team too numerous to mention. Special thanks to the early adopter critical few: Rex Brown, Dennis Stanwood, Joe Beilein, Jim LaVictoire, Patty Duetting, Kent Houston, Dan Terry, Dave Myers, Price Powell, Trevor Boagie, and Alan Meeker. They took a chance on the Advantage business model. And then followed the heavy hitters, Mike Castling, Mary Steiner, Peg Ruppert, Jeff Tucker, Kelvin Yao, Francine Smilen, Christopher Lydon, Irv Stern, and Roger Shepard.

The Advantage Performance back office. Many thanks to those who made hundreds, if not thousands, of workshops run. They made certain the materials arrived in the right configurations and the bills were sent, paid, and accounted for. The team included:

Morgan Reis, our COO, for his thoughtful and pointed business counsel. Tim Mooney, the Partner in Charge of our Evaluation and Measurement Business.

Shirley and Sheryl, the most committed and loyal client service pros imaginable, Lisa and Desiree counting the beans like they were their own, and Alex Poulsen, who made FileMaker the backbone of our business to track each project's profitability and commissions, which made sure we were viable. And our virtual marketing team, graphic designer Paula Doubleday, writing coach Laura Daly, and webmaster Julie Wolpers. The Advantage Performance Group continues to be a preeminent provider of sales and sales leadership training.

Henrik Ekelund and Jonas Ackerman. Co-founders of BTS and acquirers of our babies, Advantage Performance Group and The Real Learning Company. They are family men, with outstanding business minds with high integrity. They are hard-working and delightful company in any setting, be it business or personal. Thank you for being such great stewards of our legacy.

Special mention to the early adopters, clients who trusted us in spite of our lack of a long track record and who have spent millions with us. Ed Jennings, VP of Sales at Genentech and Chris Downey, Head of the Cell group. Richard Fuller, Tim Wallace, and Mike Benziger at Glen Ellen Winery, Craig Ramsey, Karen Neely Reed, and Kathy Grazioli at Oracle, Gary Pillete and Bruce Willson at Microsoft, and Mike Cheek, Jim Bareuther, Bob Goeddel, and Shaw Triebly at Brown Forman Beverage. Bill Doolittle and Mark Little at Kinkos, and Peter Kelly, Jason Anderson, Jim Doty, Tom Giles, and Russ Paterra at Pacific Pulmonary Services. Finally, we can never forget Fred Johnson who gave us our very first order. These people and brands helped establish Advantage as a formidable provider of sales training.

To the Advantage Alliance Partners. Warren Kurzrock and Porter Henry, our first partner. Walter Johnson, Margareta Barchan, and Klaus Melander of Celemi, Phil Geldart and Alex Somos of Eagles Flight, Sam Reese and David Pearson at Miller Heiman, Neil Rackham, Walt Zelinski, Rick Beller, and Scott Edinger at Huthwaite, Randy Root and Jim Haudan, Rich Berens, Gary Magenta and Carl Wagner of Root Learning, Howard and Sally Stevens of HR Chally Group and GrowthPlay Company, Garry Shirts of Simulation Training Systems, Don Jones at Experience IT, Grand Lum of Accordence, Brent Snow of 10,000 Feet, Alan Fine, Kim Capps, and Craig Guindon of InsideOut Development.

Authors and sales consultants extraordinaire, Nick Miller, of Clarity Advantage, and Leo Pusateri of Pusateri Consulting, who have a passion for the sales profession. Their counsel in writing my first book and their friendship over three decades is invaluable.

Special thanks to Dan Baldwin, ghostwriter, co-author, and novelist, for his insight and comments throughout the production of this work.

Epilogue

The journey to create this remarkable program began with a powerful realization one December morning many years ago. The weather was icy cold, but the weather wasn't nearly as cold as the knot in the pit of my stomach as I stood, nervously, in the windowless basement of a Windsor Ontario Holiday Inn.

At the ripe old age of 28, I had never run a seminar in my life, yet I was about to kick off and deliver a two-day seminar for a large automotive wheel manufacturing facility, a group of men older and more experienced in their profession than I in my chosen field. The crowd was, to say the least, restive. The no-smoking-until-regularly-scheduled-breaks rule was in force, which dampened the meager enthusiasm expressed by a few of the attendees. To make matters worse, the company had held its annual Christmas party the night before. Within moments, it became painfully obvious that most of my audience suffered from hangovers. My equally obvious youth and apparent inexperience did not have a calming effect on the half-ill, half-skeptical group.

My presentation required a significant amount of pre-work from each attendee. A few words here and there, a few questions, and a few poorly phrased and inadequately researched answers showed quickly and painfully that virtually everyone in the audience had passed on this essential responsibility. As the Native Americans out West say, this put an extra-heavy load in my burden basket. My dad had told me, "If a man can sell, he'll never be out of a job." So that's what I decided to do—go out there and sell my ideas, my program, and myself.

The rest of the day flew by. Hangovers, if not forgotten, were at least overshadowed and overpowered by a deep interest in the workshop. Little did I know, that event would be the first of more than 600 days spent in front of sales teams facilitating such intense (and rewarding) workshops. What had been a cold day had turned into a warm reception from an appreciative audience.

This experience had a profound influence on my thinking about training design, thinking reinforced by the VP of Product Development at Xerox Learning Systems (XLS). Derwin Fox was an aeronautical engineer who became an instructional designer. Derwin was a wise man in ways beyond his considerable academic skills. He told me three things about good instructional design.

One: Building a great training program wasn't about what content you decide to put into the program; *it was about deciding what content should be left out.* He called it elegant design. Teach a single concept, the core message of the workshop that immediately strikes home and stays with people long after the seminar. It should be memorable and repeatable. Dr. Garry Shirts, another friend, mentor, and guru of simulation design, called designing "to capture the essence."

Two: The look and feel of the materials has an immediate impact on the learner. The look of the presentation materials validates or invalidates the material within. It's reminiscent of a well-known sales adage. Regardless of how wonderful the steak may be; you still sell the sizzle. Packaging provides that sizzle. If the materials look home-grown or slipshod, the attendee automatically assumes the information is the same quality. The audience develops negative feelings before the program even begins. They may not even realize those feelings, or articulate them but they're still in place and damaging your presentation. Derwin believed strongly in powerful package design for training products and he definitely built the Xerox training brand around that philosophy.

Three: The best way to judge any training program is how quickly you hear people putting a common language into play. I like to hear them using the language I've taught by the first break of the morning of the first session I teach.

Level Five Selling meets all of Derwin's criteria. It is an elegant, simple model that is memorable and repeatable. Apply it and have immediate "Day One" results. I am delighted to have shared the Level Five Selling model with you and I hope it pays you many dividends in satisfied customers, above-quota performance, and pride in being a part of the world's greatest profession. I'll say this—it won't leave you out in the cold.

About the Author

John began his career selling sales and sales leadership training with Xerox Learning Systems. First appointed an account executive in the firm's Toronto office, he was subsequently named regional sales manager, general sales manager, and, ultimately, Director of U.S. Sales Operations.

Next, John joined Omega Performance, an international bank consulting firm, as EVP Sales and Marketing.

Then, together with two partners, John founded Advantage Performance Group and The Real Learning Company, a human performance management venture that grew to a national network of more than 75 performance consultants serving 300 clients. This business realized $24 million when acquired by a Stockholm-based public multinational.

John has sold or oversaw the sale of more than $350 million of licensed training, and today his practice is focused exclusively on the sales function. His work includes executive coaching, developing sales management processes, sales forecast management, salesforce assessment and recruiting, new product launch, sales talent development, and sales coaching.

Praise for John Hoskins

Combines a lifetime of sales leadership experience with a keen ability to top grade learning concepts.
Kim Capps, CEO, InsideOut Development

In the field of sales leadership and development, John Hoskins has seen and done it all. You would be hard pressed to find a greater resource and expert in this space.
Leo Pusateri, President & Owner of Pusateri Consulting, and author of *Mirror Mirror on the Wall Am I The Most Valued of Them All?* and *You Are the Value*

One of the most distinguished business professionals with whom I have had the pleasure to work. *Level Five Selling* is a direct reflection of his decades of proven experience and expertise in the field of sales effectiveness. It is also a tangible expression of his commitment to generously sharing his knowledge with others.
Rick Beller, Global President and COO, The History Factory

One of the smartest sales thinkers out there. He really gets the value of pre-call preparation.
Bobby Martin, Active Chairman & President, Vertical IQ, and author of *The Hockey Stick Principles: The 4 Key Stages to Entrepreneurial Success*

John Hoskins brings to the sales arena a fundamental clarity and simplicity that lies at the heart of all learning and peak performance.
Alan Fine, Founder and President, InsideOut Development

John Hoskins is a master at understanding the keys to outstanding human performance; he demystifies sales excellence.
Jim Haudan, CEO, Root Inc., and author of *The Art of Engagement*

An incredibly talented business executive and sales leader with decades of real-world sales experience, which he has leveraged to write an outstanding book.
Tim Owen, Founder & CEO, NeuroCrunch LLC

For more information about bulk purchase of *Level Five Selling*, or to discuss how you can train your sales team utilizing the Level Five Selling Sales Managers Kit, contact John Hoskins at:

Email: John@LevelFiveSelling.com

Website: LevelFiveSelling.com

Call or Text: 480.235.5582

Other books available on Amazon by Level Five Selling

 Level Five Selling is for sales leaders who want to dramatically increase their odds of exceeding their quota year after year. However, it is equally relevant for sales trainers, who want to increase the certainty of a payback on the training programs they build or buy. Finally, it also applies to sales representatives who seek to master the art of selling, earn top commissions, and enjoy the recognition associated with being number one on the sales leader board.

 The Level Five Coaching System provides a road map for sales enablement managers and sales leaders to follow when implementing a documented and fully implemented process for coaching and developing preeminent sales teams. This system provides the frontline sales leaders with the method, skills, tools, and resources to execute dynamic coaching. In addition, this book offers a step-by-step formula and specific "how to's" for any sized sales organization to improve win rates, reduce turnover, reduce ramp to productivity time, and meet and exceed your top-line revenue targets.

 If a company expects its sales leaders to meet or exceed its revenue goals, they must be outstanding recruiters, trainers, and coaches. So, we wrote **The Level Five Sales Leader** to share our insights gained from our combined decades of sales consulting experience, helping sales leaders to achieve that goal. If you focus on these critical success factors of frontline sales leaders. In that case, we firmly believe you will see dramatic improvements in sales results, less turnover, higher win rates, and more satisfied and loyal customers.

 Sales leaders who consistently perform at the top of their game are collaborative coaches and outstanding communicators.

If you fail to:

- Understand your sales professional's point of view; you stand little chance of winning them to your point of view.
- Explicitly call attention to your sales professional's strengths, progress, and successes; you squander opportunities to encourage more positive behavior.
- Clearly and directly express disagreement or calling out counter-productive behavior or performance, you deny your sales professionals the information they need to make progress.

On the other hand, if you establish and maintain collaborative coaching relationships with your salespeople and invite innovation, they flourish.

Contact Us   You can bulk purchase the books at a discount by contacting us. To learn more about how Level Five Selling helps frontline sales leaders become masterful sales coaches, please contact us at info@levelfiveselling.com or 800-975-6768 David Pearson Ext 701 John Hoskins Ext 702. www.levelfiveselling.com.

We would welcome a call to discuss your needs.